M shed

Souvenir Guide

Introducing M Shed

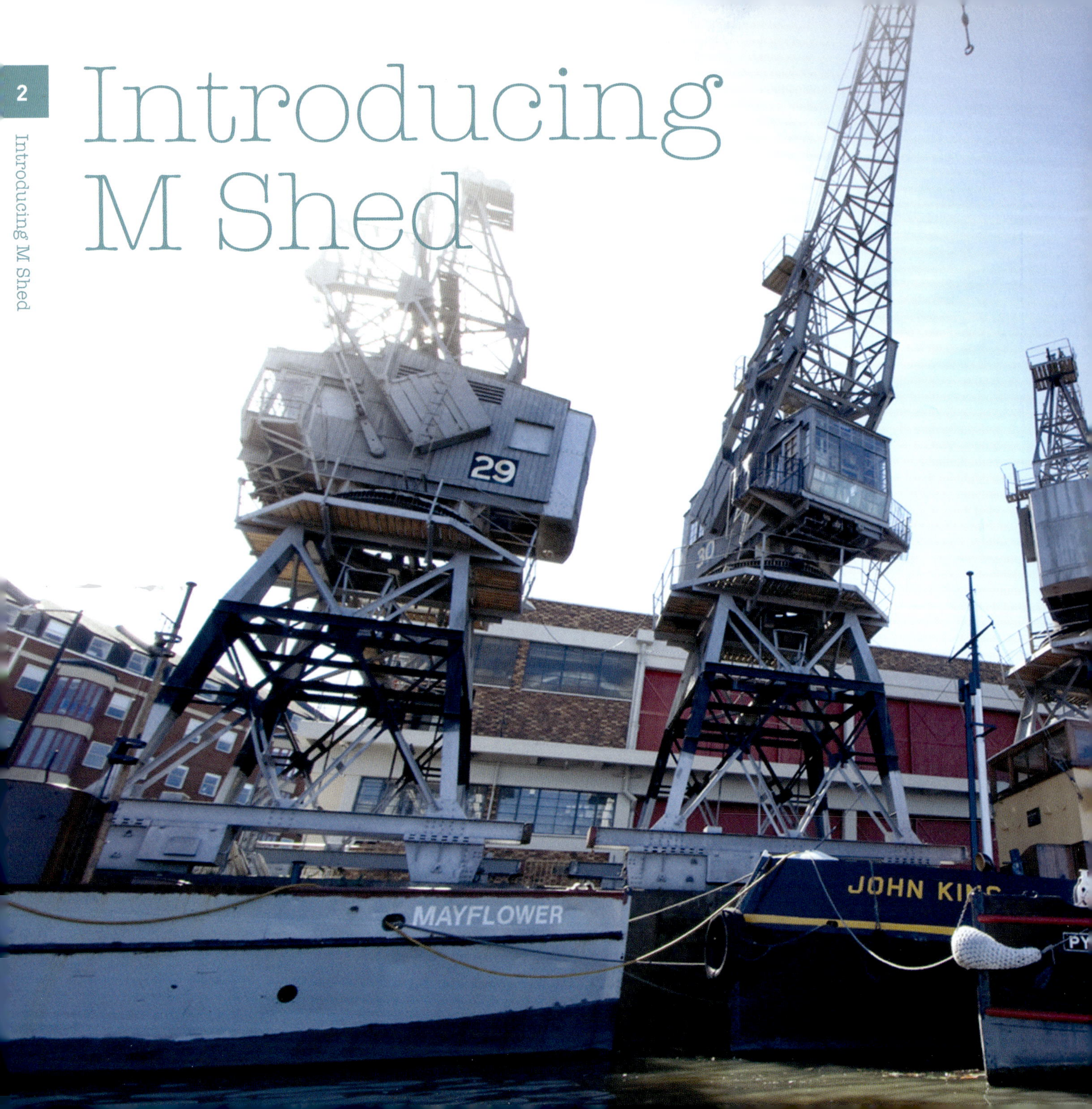

This landmark museum offers many stories about the extraordinary lives of ordinary people and Bristol's connections with the wider world. It captures the very essence of what makes Bristol the city that it is today and sparks conversations about its past, present and future.

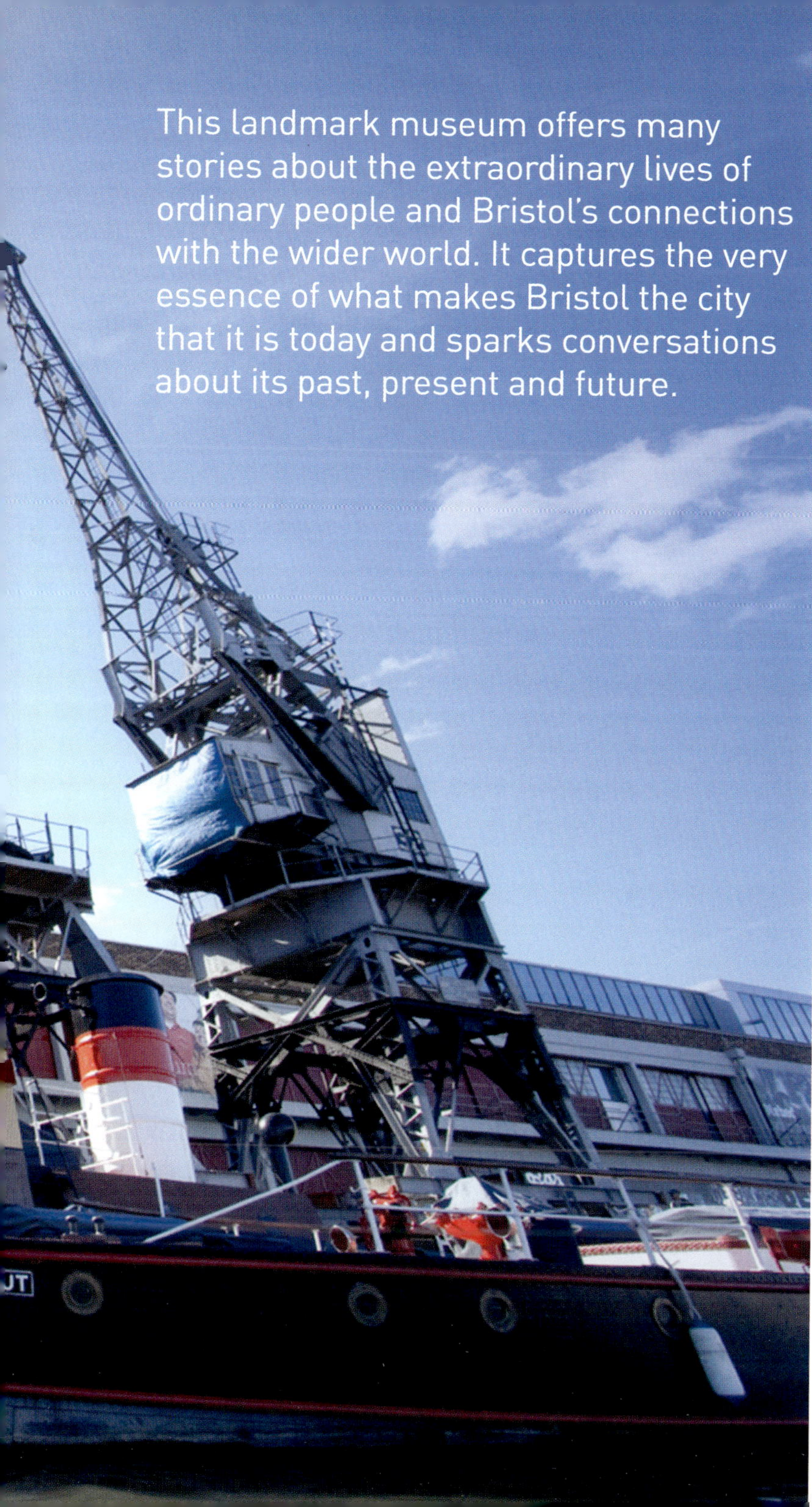

© Chris Bahn

M Shed's galleries, housed in a former dockside transit shed, are rich in iconic objects and works of art, documents, photographs, films and personal testimonies. They reveal the place, its people and their daily lives, through stories of industry and invention, of family and factories, of immigration and slavery, and of celebration and hardship. Outside, its trains, boats and cranes, which are among the last remnants of the working dockside, are considered as much a part of the museum as its galleries. M Shed encourages visitors to go out and explore the living city.

This book highlights just some of those objects and stories that M Shed uses to unlock Bristol and its secrets, and acts as a signpost for further exploration.

Inside...

M Shed: Harbourside

Bristol's success as a city was largely due to its thriving port.

Bristol has existed for over a thousand years. Its position in the landscape, relative to the River Frome and the River Avon, which provided access to and from the Severn, made it an ideal place for trading locally, nationally and then internationally.

For many years the port that developed here was the beating heart of the city. Ships sailed right up into the centre of Bristol to dock and unload their goods, before setting sail again with cargo bound for other countries.

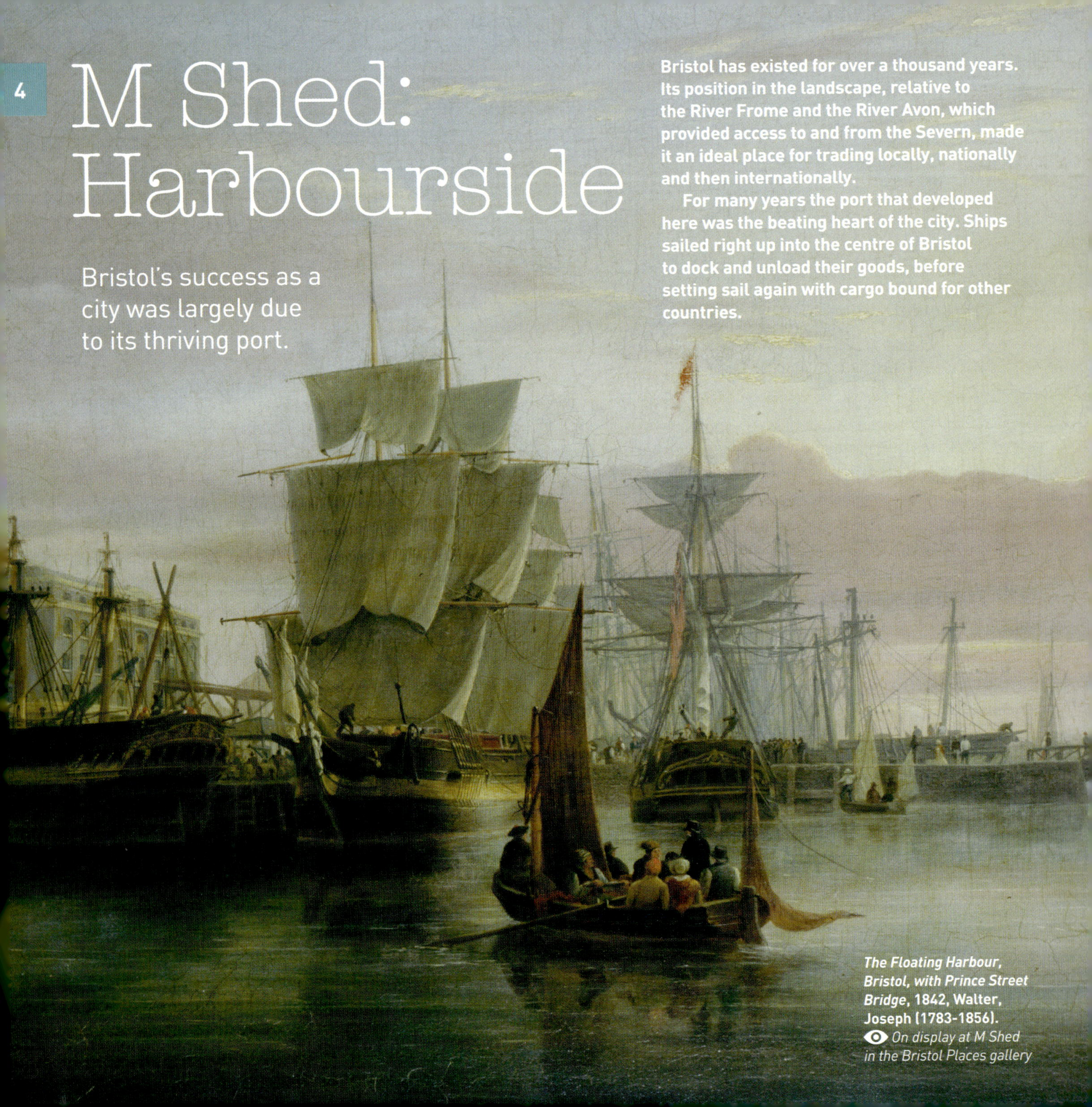

***The Floating Harbour, Bristol, with Prince Street Bridge*, 1842, Walter, Joseph (1783-1856).**
On display at M Shed in the Bristol Places gallery

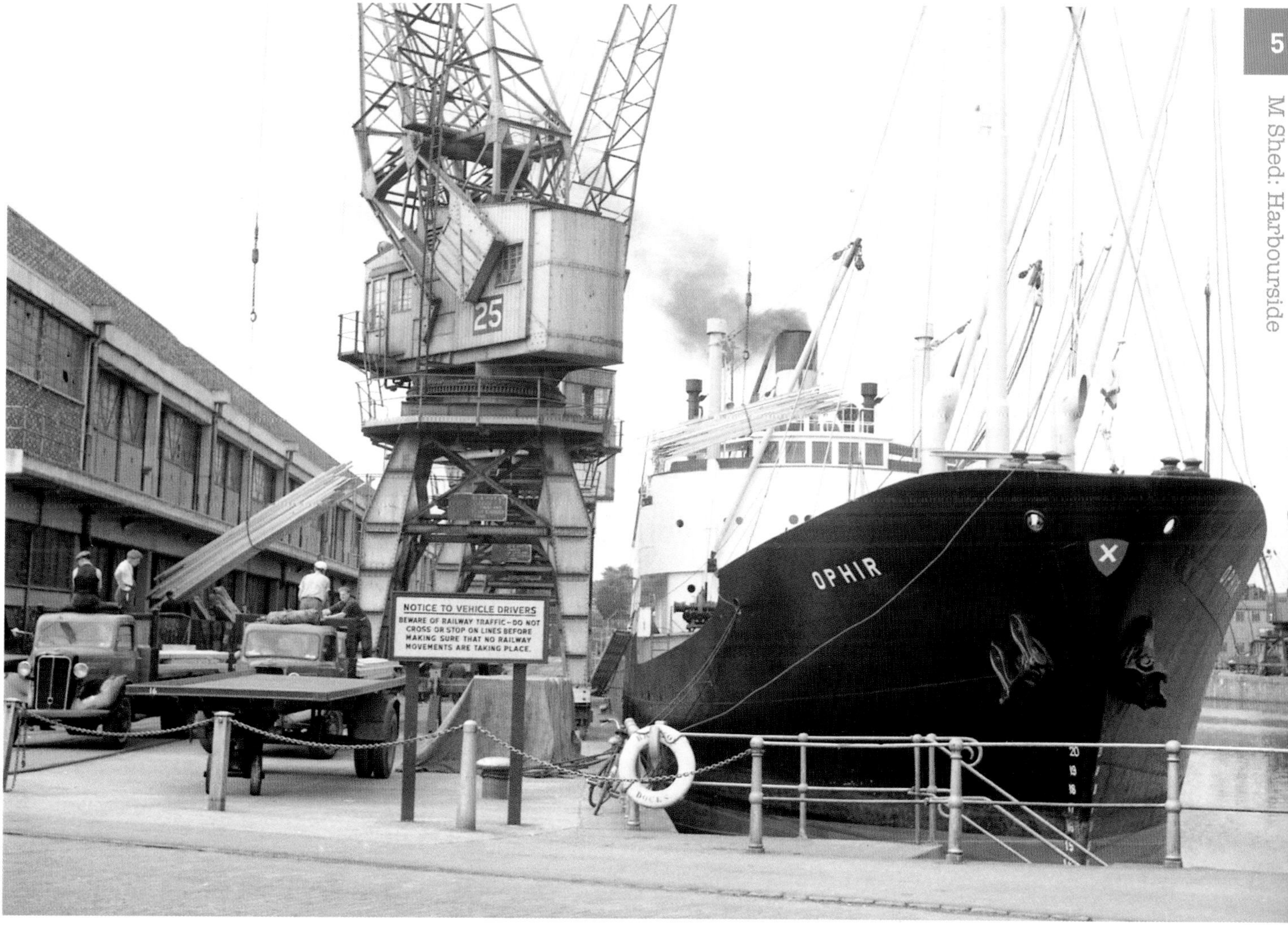

Vessel 'Ophir' unloading timber from USSR at M Shed and L Shed, 1955.

Bristol's original docksides looked quite different to those we see today. A deep trench was dug in the 1200s to create a new deeper harbour. In 1809 it was transformed once again by the opening of the Floating Harbour. Sadly, by the late 1960s the city-centre docks were in decline and finally closed to commercial shipping in 1975. However, the remnants of what was once a thriving busy port can still be seen on Princes Wharf where M Shed stands today. Its towering cranes winched huge crates of cargo from vessels docked at the quayside onto waiting lorries, railway wagons, barges or forklift trucks, to be stored in a transit shed or for distribution around the country.

M Shed, which is now the museum, is one of those transit sheds. Two large state-of-the-art general cargo sheds, 'L' and 'M', were built on Princes Wharf after World War II to cope with the post-war trade. The first ships arrived in 1952. These sheds are the last in the line of many other buildings that have occupied the site.

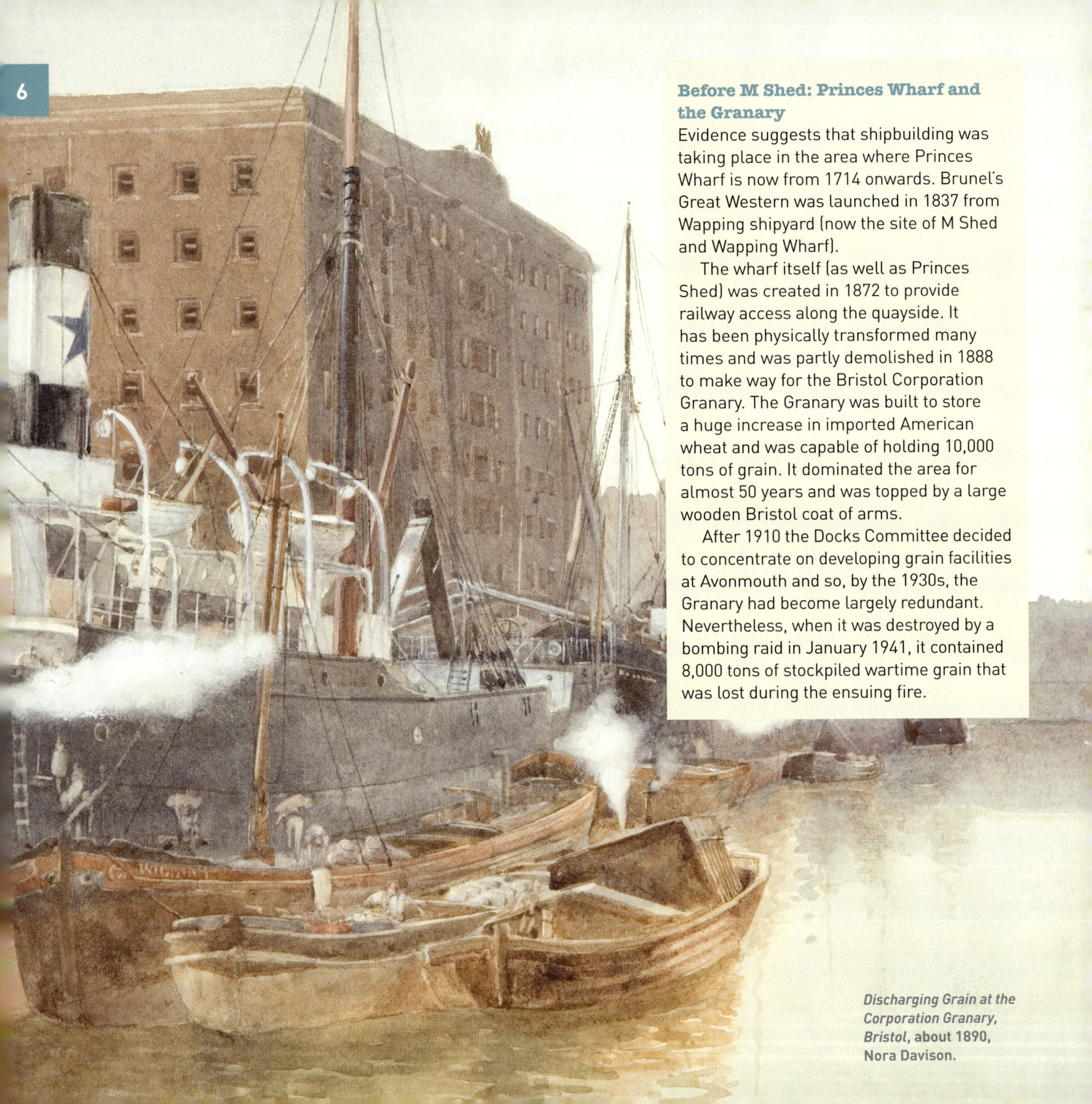

Before M Shed: Princes Wharf and the Granary

Evidence suggests that shipbuilding was taking place in the area where Princes Wharf is now from 1714 onwards. Brunel's *Great Western* was launched in 1837 from Wapping shipyard (now the site of M Shed and Wapping Wharf).

The wharf itself (as well as Princes Shed) was created in 1872 to provide railway access along the quayside. It has been physically transformed many times and was partly demolished in 1888 to make way for the Bristol Corporation Granary. The Granary was built to store a huge increase in imported American wheat and was capable of holding 10,000 tons of grain. It dominated the area for almost 50 years and was topped by a large wooden Bristol coat of arms.

After 1910 the Docks Committee decided to concentrate on developing grain facilities at Avonmouth and so, by the 1930s, the Granary had become largely redundant. Nevertheless, when it was destroyed by a bombing raid in January 1941, it contained 8,000 tons of stockpiled wartime grain that was lost during the ensuing fire.

***Discharging Grain at the Corporation Granary, Bristol*, about 1890, Nora Davison.**

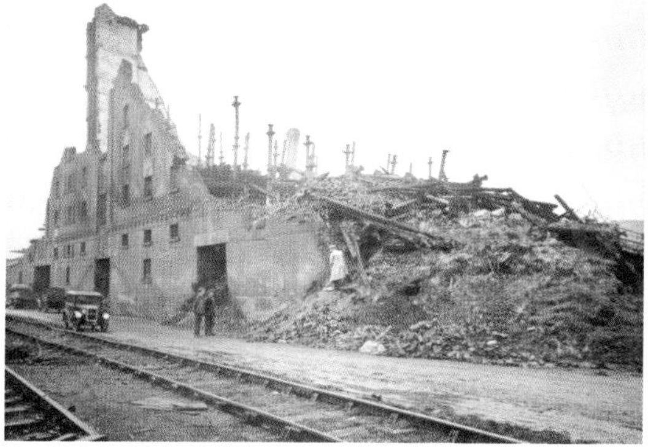
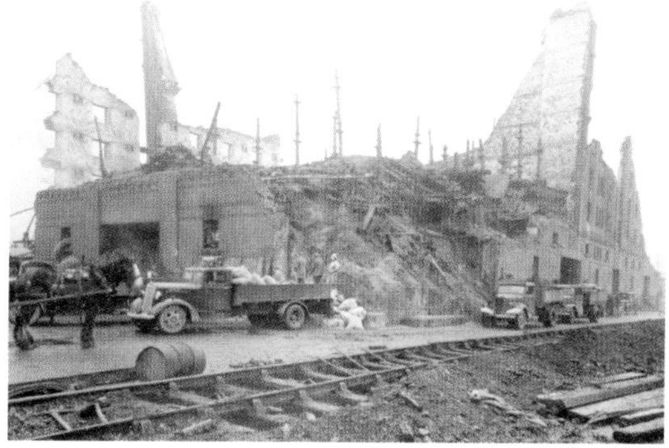

The remains of the Corporation Granary after it was bombed in 1941.

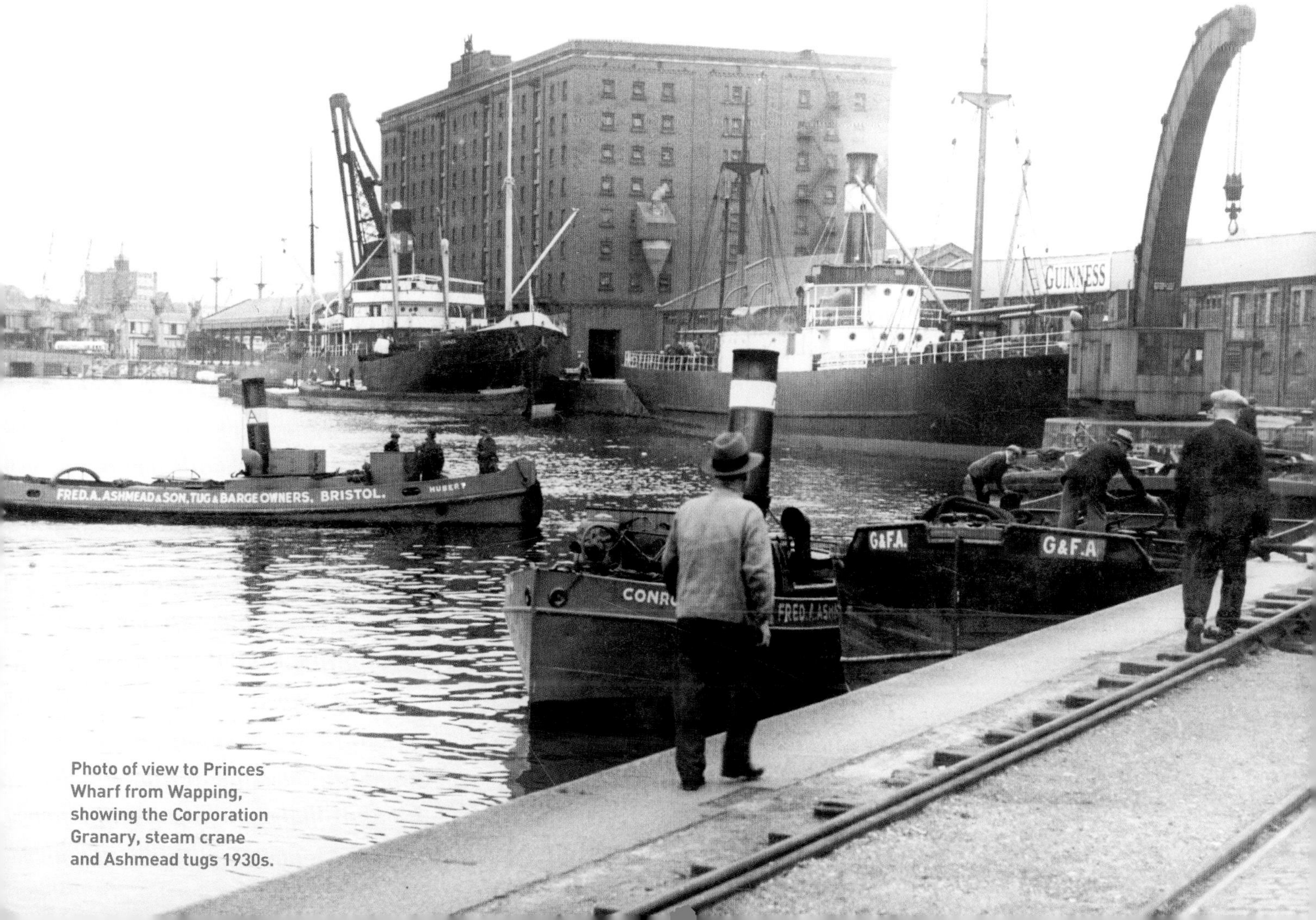

Photo of view to Princes Wharf from Wapping, showing the Corporation Granary, steam crane and Ashmead tugs 1930s.

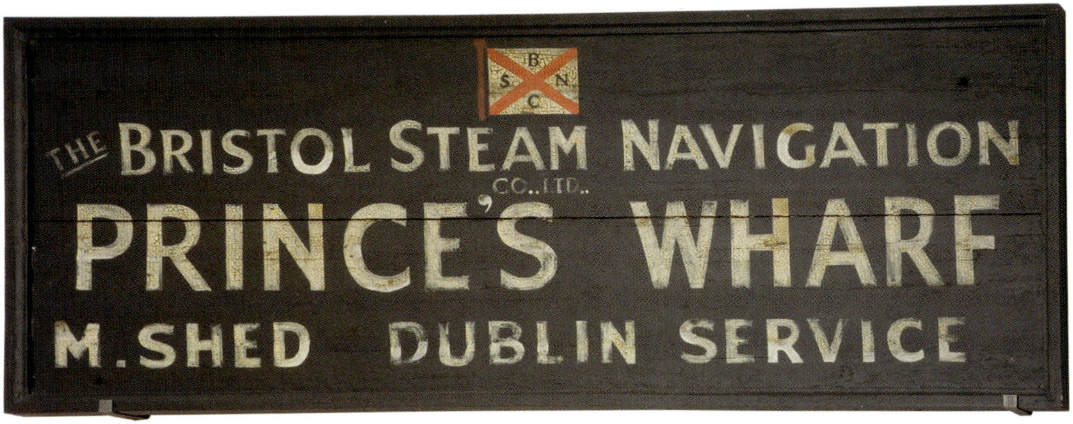

Painted wooden sign (left) formerly fixed to the rear of M Shed advertising the Bristol Steam Navigation Co., Princes Wharf, M Shed Dublin Service. 1954.
On display in the Bristol Places gallery

The Echo (below, left) was one of the ships that the Bristol Steam Navigation Company used to trade to M Shed. She was converted to carry containers in the mid-1960s, a sign of a big change in the shipping industry. Scale 1:64.
On display in the Bristol Places gallery

This plaque (below) records the opening of Bristol Industrial Museum in 1978. The museum was open for 28 years and closed in 2006 so that it could be redeveloped as a new museum – M Shed which opened in 2011.
On display in the Bristol Places gallery

M Shed

The buildings that were constructed on Princes Wharf in the 1950s, L Shed and M Shed, formed part of a purpose built general cargo wharf. Many of the dockside warehouses and facilities were named after letters of the alphabet.

M Shed was used primarily by the Bristol Steam Navigation Company for its twice-weekly cargo service to Dublin. It was a temporary storage facility for bacon, potatoes, beef, butter and Guinness. The company pioneered the use of shipping containers on this site before moving to Avonmouth in 1969.

The docks were finally closed as a commercial entity in 1975, following a period of gradual decline. In 1978, the fortunes of Princes Wharf were revived when M Shed and L Shed were converted into Bristol Industrial Museum and a general museum collections' store. Between 1979 and 1988, L Shed was also home to the National Lifeboat Museum.

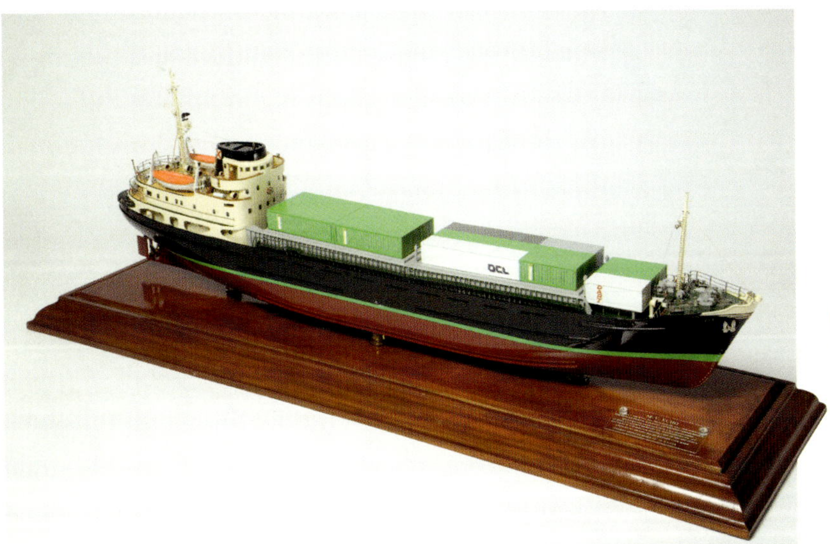

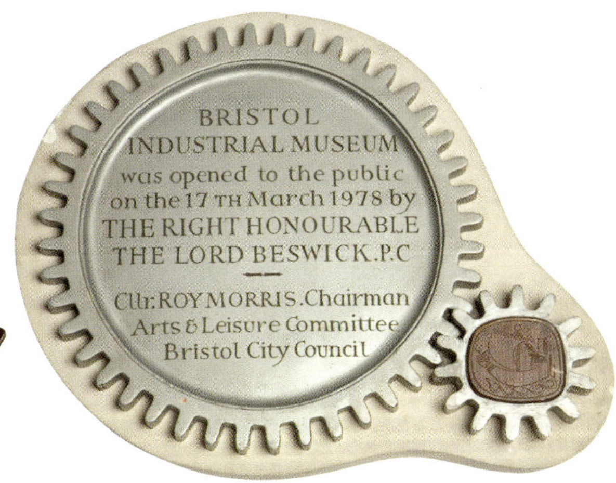

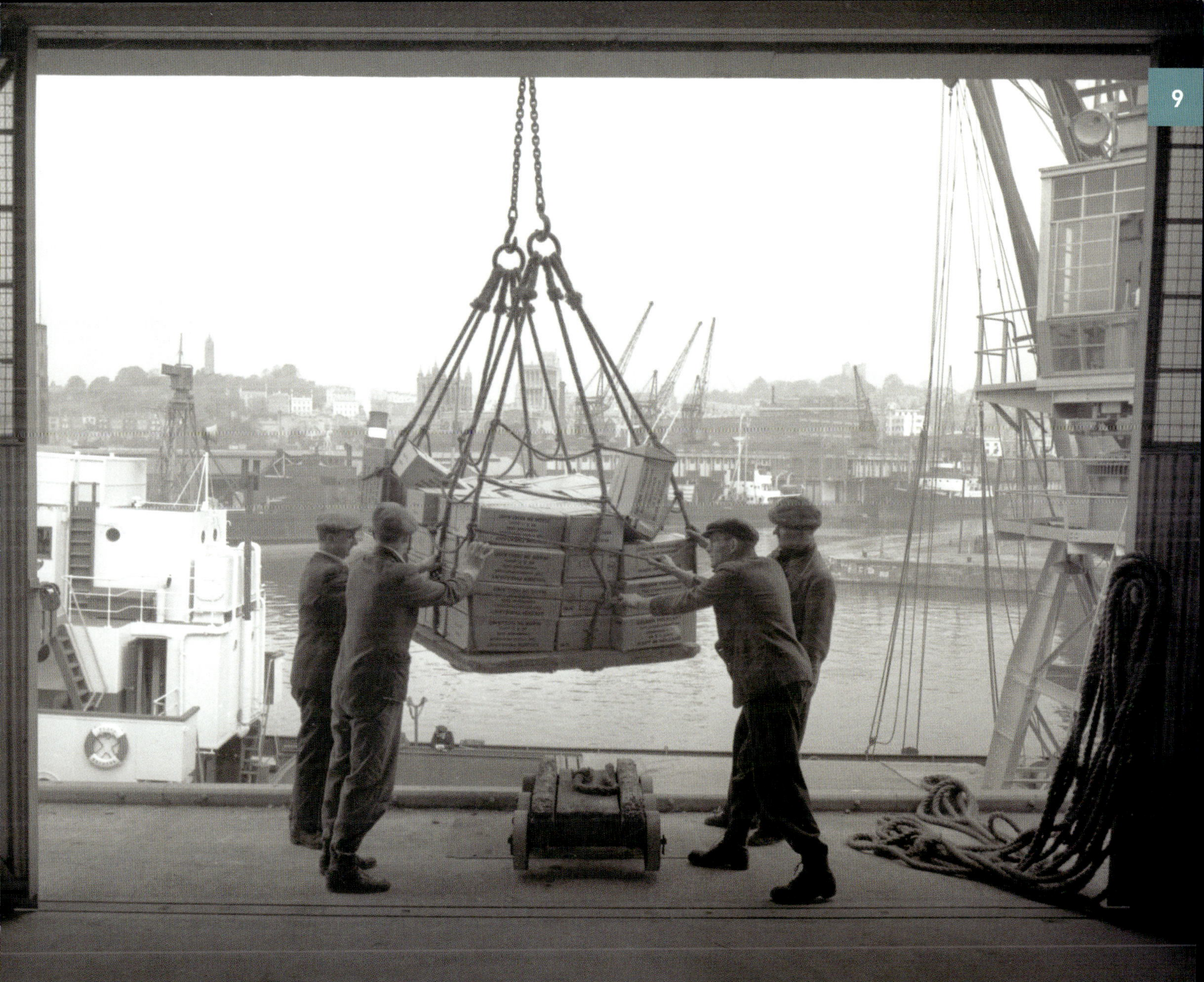

“We thought the docks would go on forever... there'd be huge ships from all over the world, dockers everywhere, and cargo being loaded on and off. It's a way of life which has now disappeared.”

Jim Dallimore, who worked at the City Docks during the 1960s

Dockers receiving a tray of crated condensed milk from the Bristol Steam Navigation Company ship into the first floor of L Shed.

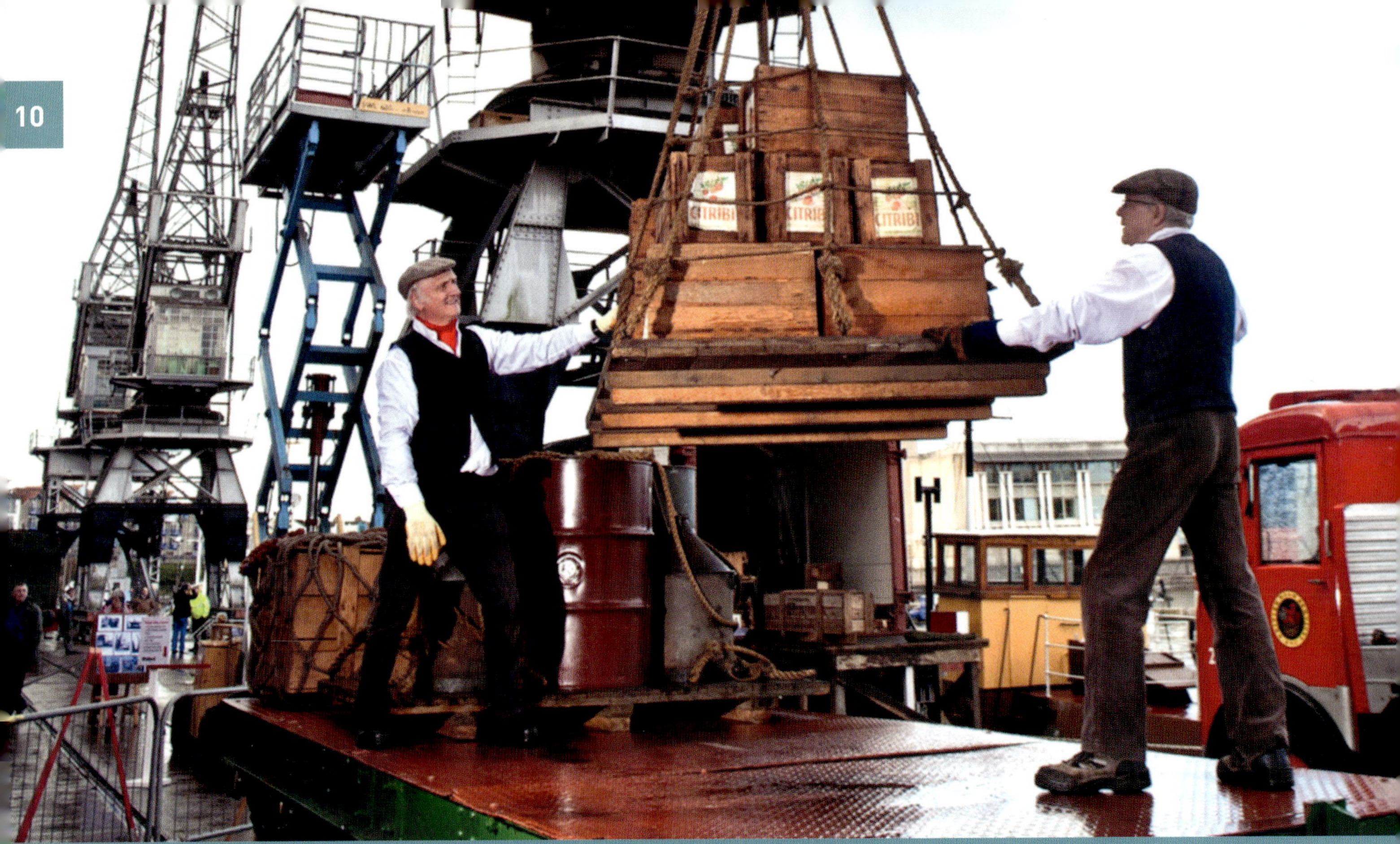

© Neil Phillips

Trains, boats and cranes

M Shed's iconic working exhibits provide a lasting reminder of a hustling, bustling and busy working dockside. They are often in demand to provide the setting for period films and TV. However, many of these exhibits pre-date M Shed and one is even designated as a Scheduled Ancient Monument.

M Shed's trains, boats and cranes are kept in working order by volunteers. They also bring them to life most weekends for trips and especially during Docks Heritage Weekend.

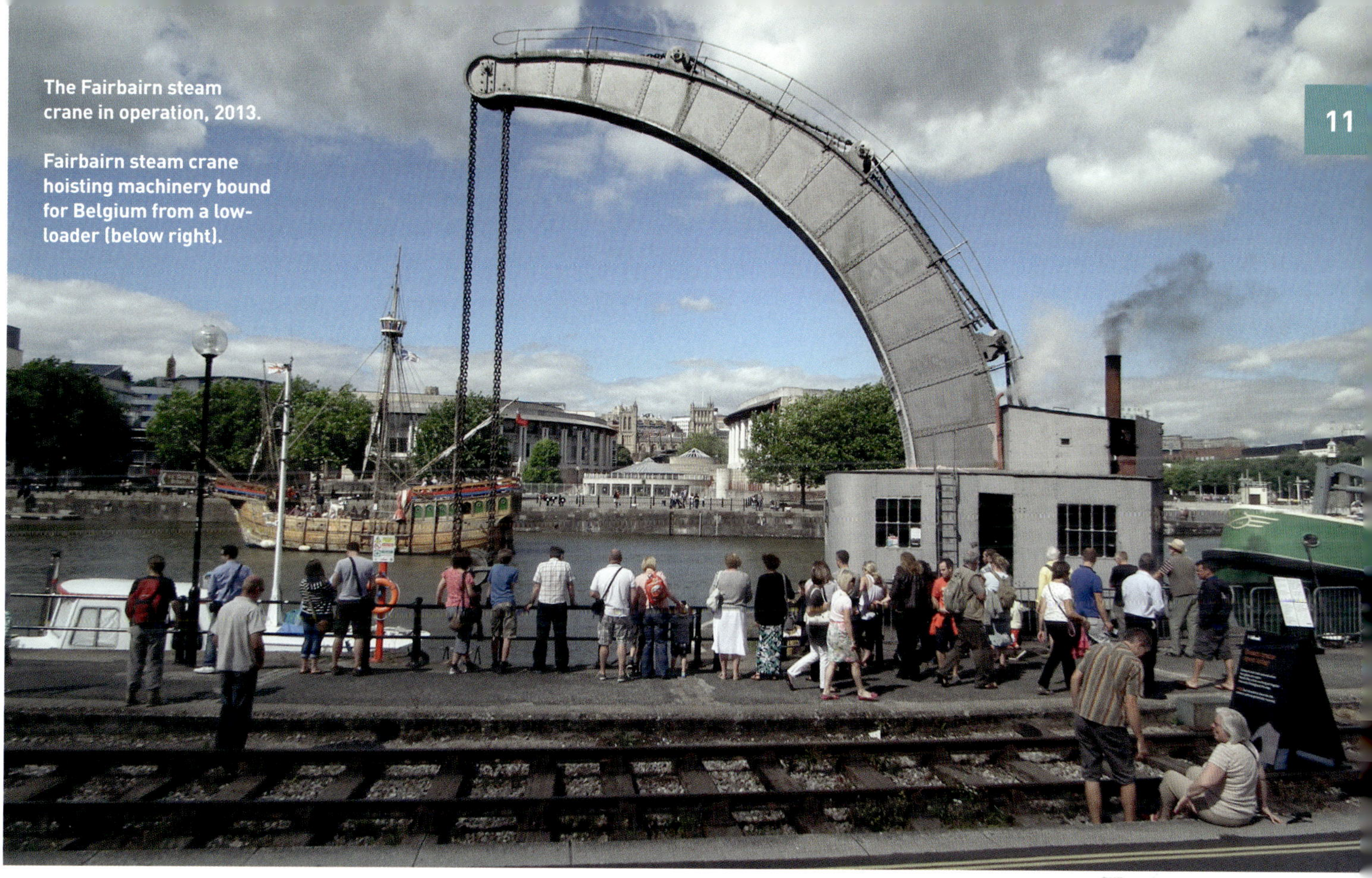

The Fairbairn steam crane in operation, 2013.

Fairbairn steam crane hoisting machinery bound for Belgium from a low-loader (below right).

Early cranes

Cranes have been a feature of Bristol's dockside since 1472 when Alice Chestre, the widow of a Bristol draper and a successful businesswoman, donated £41 to pay for the first one in the harbour. Others followed: in 1733, John Padmore, a Bristol engineer and famous designer of cranes, constructed the 'Great Crane' which became a tourist attraction. This crane sat on the western side of the Mud Dock (opposite M Shed) "erected on 14 pillars of cast Iron... a curious piece of Mechanism, and worthy of observation" (Matthews Directory 1794).

In the 1870s, the Docks Engineer Thomas Howard arranged the building of the Fairbairn steam crane, which is now the sole survivor of its type in the world and a Scheduled Ancient Monument. It was built by Stothert & Pitt in 1878, to a design by Sir William Fairbairn to lift heavy loads (up to 35.56 tonnes) from the deep holds of ships. Although it was used only occasionally throughout most of its working life, it was kept busy day and night during World War II, handling assault landing craft.

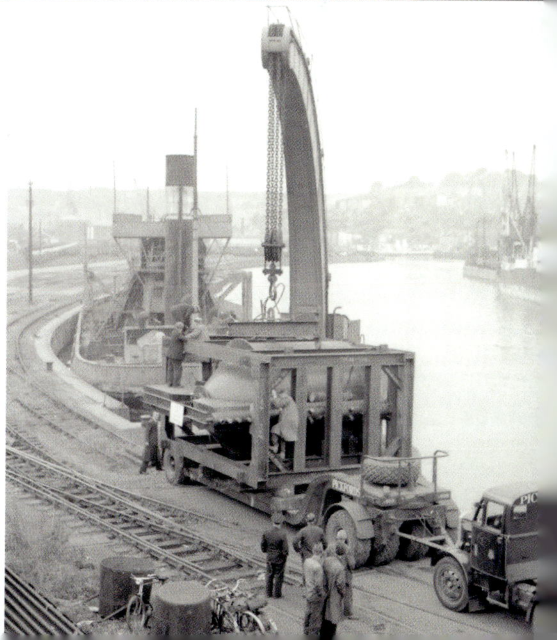

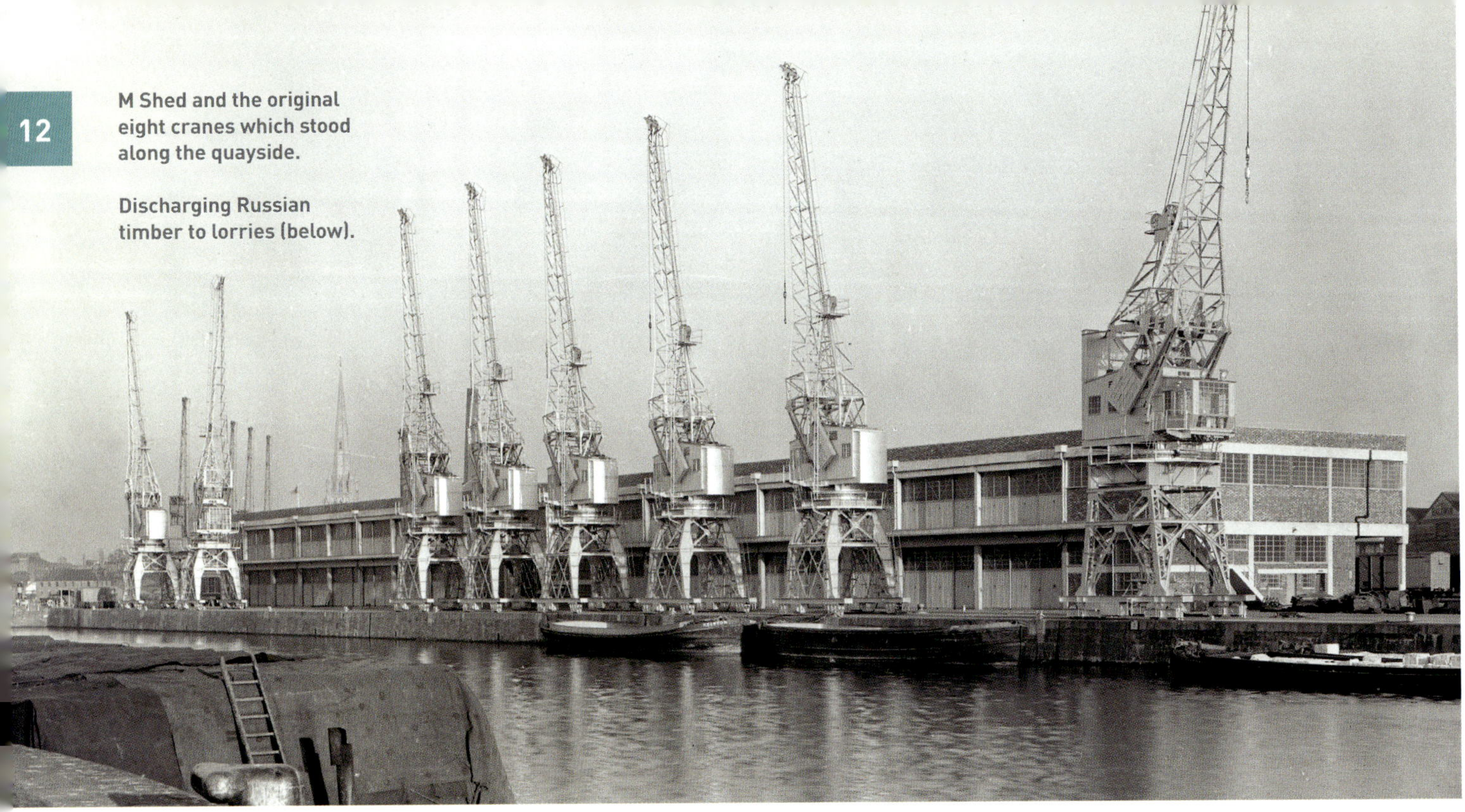

M Shed and the original eight cranes which stood along the quayside.

Discharging Russian timber to lorries (below).

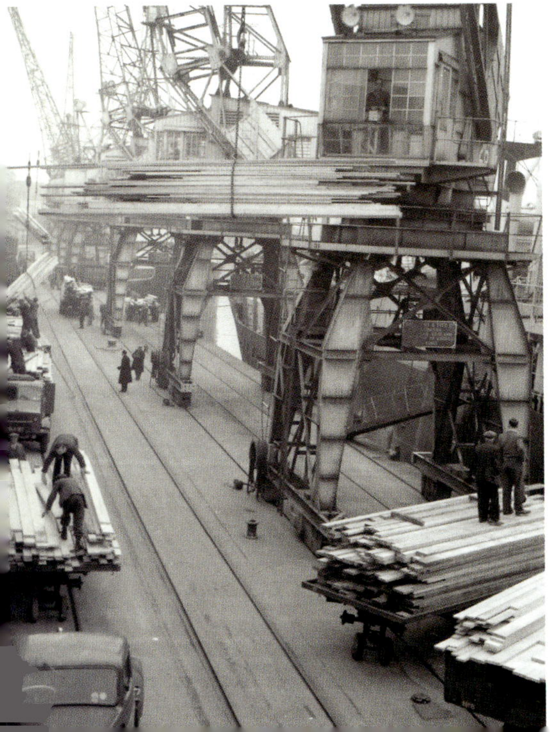

Electric cranes

The four cargo cranes that sit beside M Shed are the biggest objects in the whole of the museum's collection: they are the last survivors of eight that sat on the quayside here, and of over 40 as a whole in the City Docks during the 1950s.

They were not the first electric cranes to be built in Bristol's harbour, since they had begun to appear here as early as the late 1800s, and one was installed in the railway goods shed in 1906. Those you can see today were all made by Stothert & Pitt in Bath, an engineering company that pioneered the use of electricity to drive cranes and which specialised in dockside models like these. The cranes are able to move along the dock edge on their own rails and were generally designed to lift between two and five tons. Their design enabled them to work side by side in close proximity over the same ship's hold which helped them to load and unload ships as quickly as possible.

M Shed's cranes were the last to work with regular cargo before the closure of the City Docks to commercial traffic: they helped to offload the last Baltic trader to call here in November 1974. The cranes were due to be sold for scrap but two were saved by a pressure group called City Docks Ventures. Bristol City Council then bought the remaining two. All four are now owned by the council. Volunteers started to restore the cranes in 2001, and they're now able to move once again under their own power.

On the water...

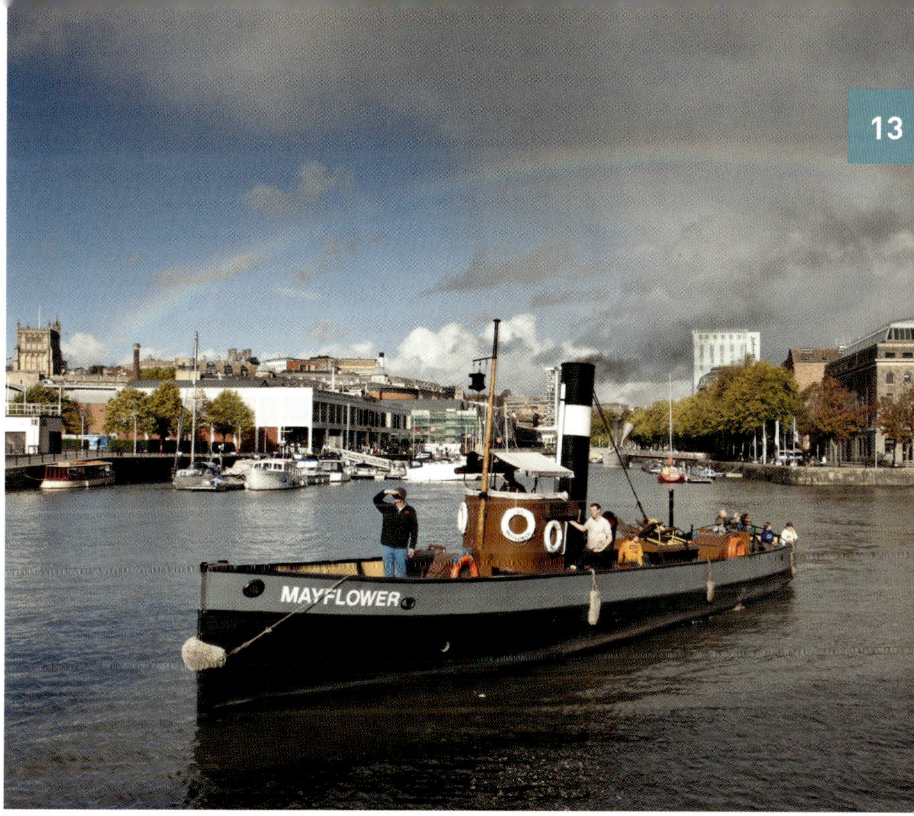

© Neil Phillips

Mayflower

Mayflower is the oldest Bristol-built ship still afloat, and the world's oldest surviving tug. This steam tug was built in 1861 by GK Stothert & Co. to work on the Gloucester & Sharpness Canal and the River Severn, but was later modified for work in the Bristol Channel. Mayflower was sold for scrap by British Waterways in 1967 but was saved from being cut up and was eventually purchased by Bristol Museum in 1981. It took a team of volunteers six years to restore Mayflower to the typical appearance of the mid-to-late 1800s.

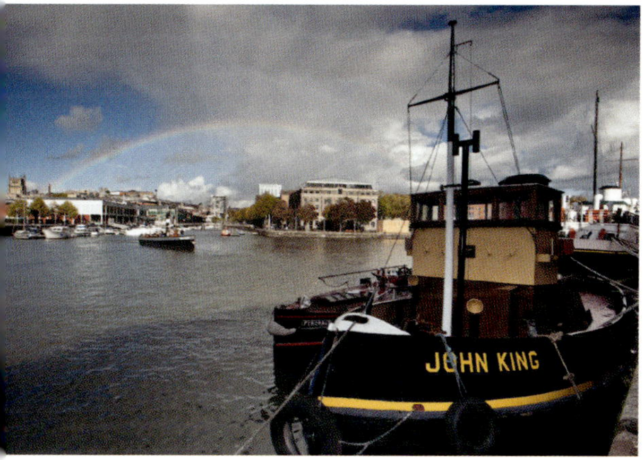

© Neil Phillips

John King

Tugs are small powerful boats used to manoeuvre large ships. Steam tugs performed this service on the river approaches to Bristol from the 1840s until diesel tugs like the John King, took over in the 1930s. The King family owned the biggest tug fleet in Bristol and the John King, launched in 1935, was named after the fleet's founder, Christopher (John) King. The tug was used to train new crews and was still in use in the 1970s before being purchased by the museum.

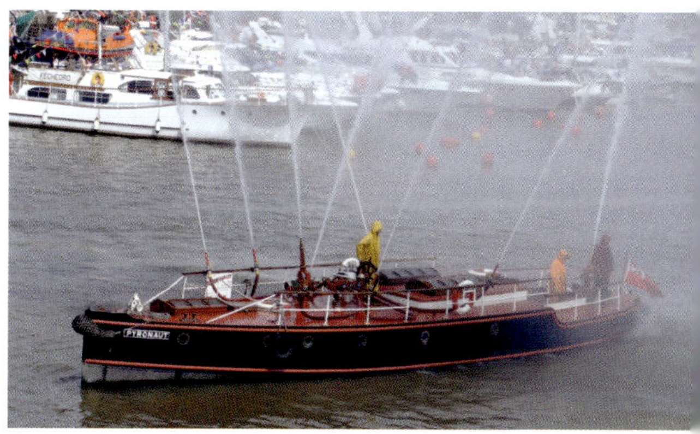

Pyronaut

Boats like Pyronaut were a vital part of Bristol's firefighting service. Built in Bristol in 1934, at Charles Hill & Sons shipyard, Pyronaut was designed to pass under every bridge in the harbour without them being opened. This made it easier to reach fires quickly. Although originally named Bristol Phoenix II, Pyronaut was renamed in 1938 and during WWII was in action every time Bristol was bombed. After the war she was used to fight several major fires and remained in service until 1973.

Harbour railway

Small railways that were used to move materials in mines and around major factories became common all over Britain after the 1860s. Bristol's first railway, the Avon & Gloucestershire Railway, opened as a horse-drawn 'dramway' in 1832. It ran from Shortwood to Avon Wharf at Keynsham and closed in the late 1860s. Another dramway, the Bristol & Gloucestershire Railway, was built to move coal from pits in Coalpit Heath to Bristol harbour at Cuckold's Pill, and opened in 1835. It quickly converted to locomotive use and became part of the Midland Railway.

The Bristol Harbour Railway was a goods line of the Great Western Railway. When it was built in 1872, it came from the goods yard at Temple Meads. It then went through a tunnel under St Mary Redcliffe churchyard, over a steam-powered lifting bridge outside the Ostrich pub on Bathurst Basin, and on to Princes Wharf, at the back of M Shed. Later it was extended onto Wapping Wharf, to where the SS Great Britain is docked today.

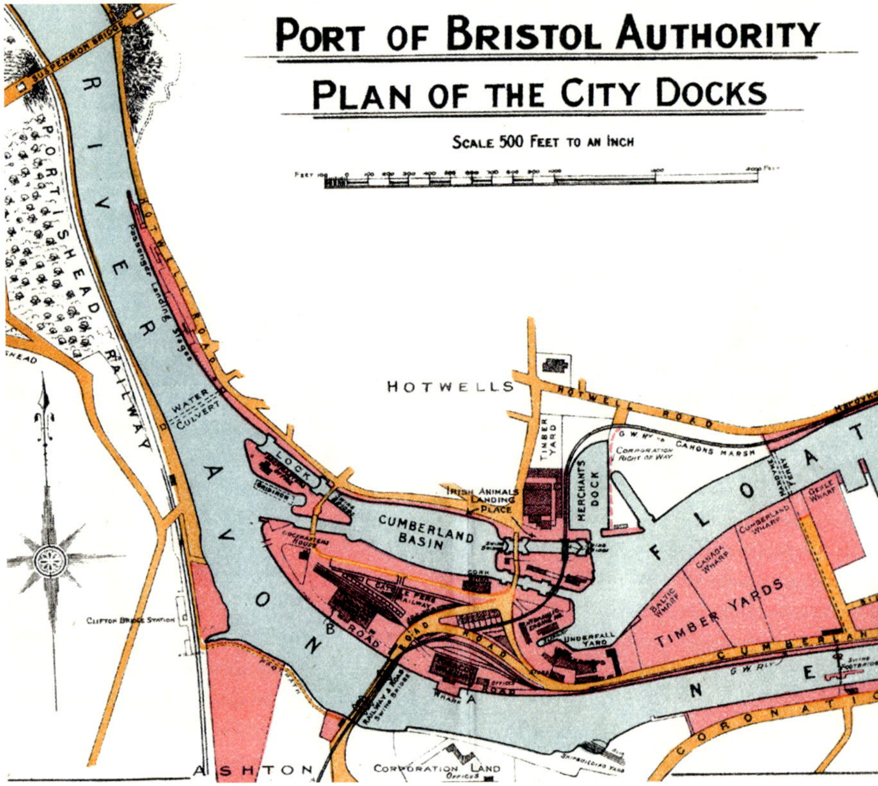

© Neil Phillips

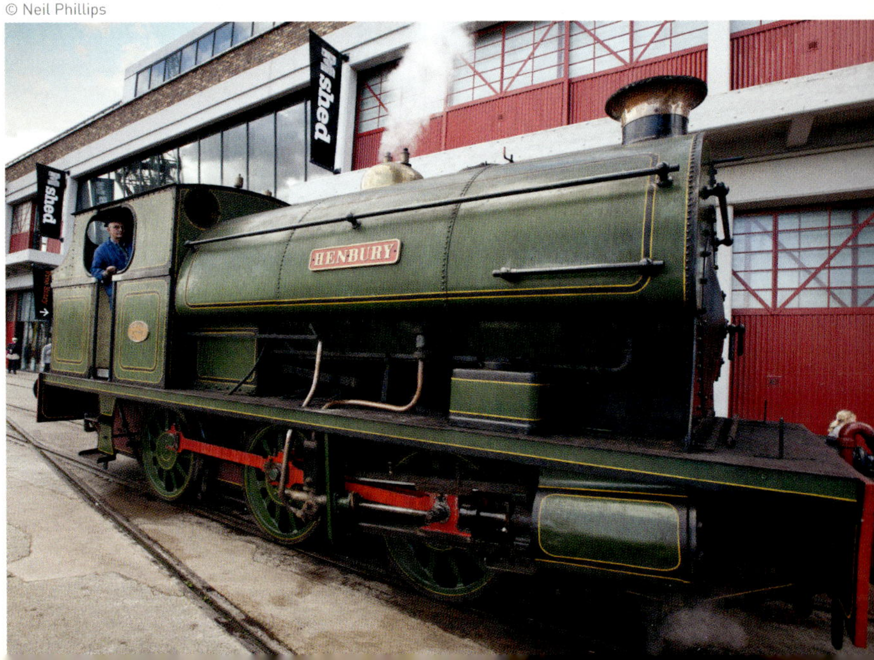

On the rails...

Henbury

Henbury was built in 1937 by Thomas Peckett & Sons in Speedwell, Bristol.

This engine was part of a large fleet of steam locomotives working at the docks at Avonmouth. The port's locomotive crews kept her in good working order until diesel engines took over in the early 1960s.

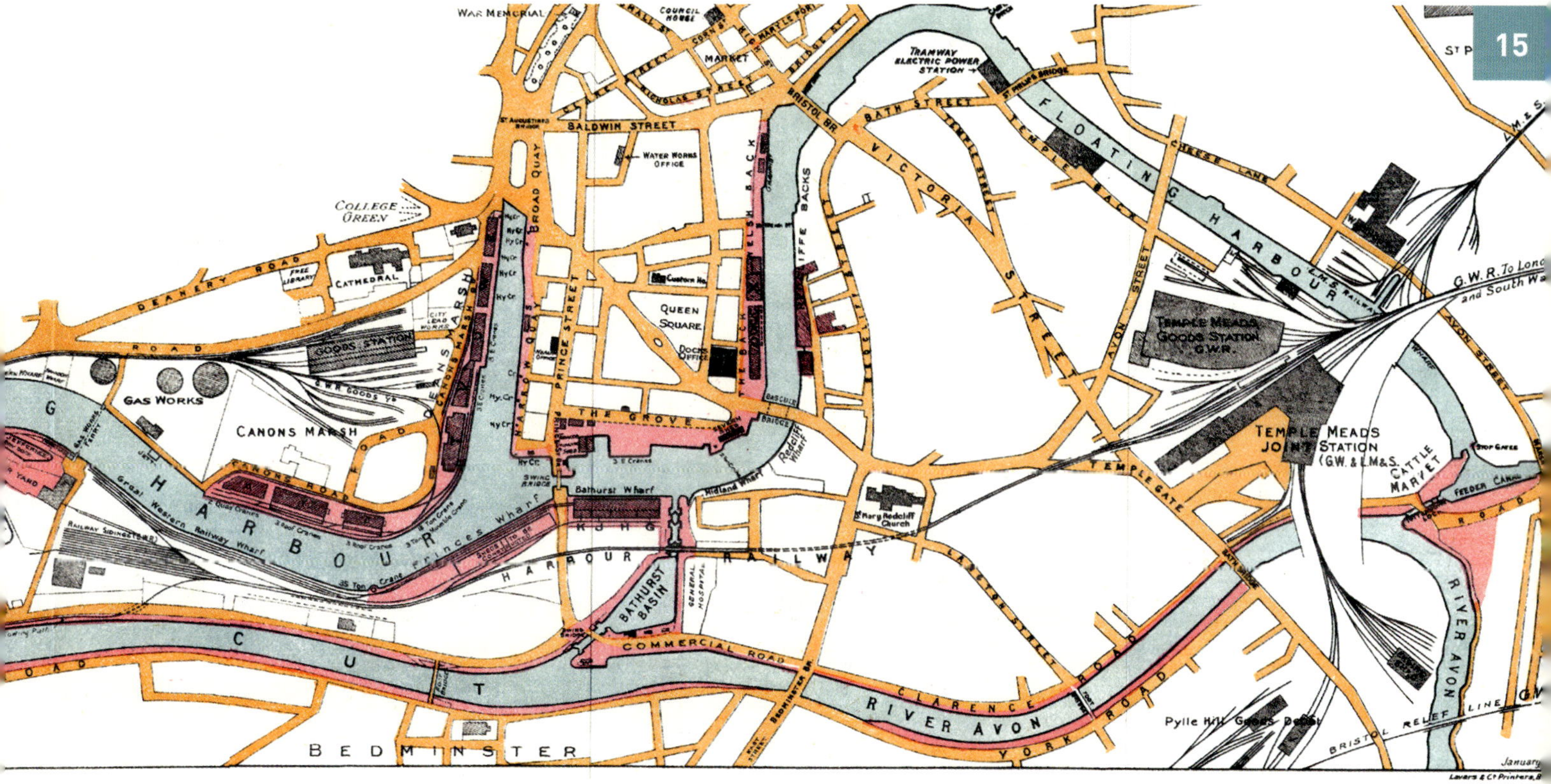

Plan of the City Docks showing the harbour railway line, 1950.
See a large version of this map on show in M Shed's West End Foyer

Portbury

Portbury was built by the Avonside Engine Company Ltd at Fishponds, Bristol, in 1917.

This battleship-grey engine worked on the construction of the new Portbury shipyard during World War I. From there she was moved to the Avonmouth Docks on the opposite side of the River Avon where she was often used to pull loads much greater than she was originally specified to carry.

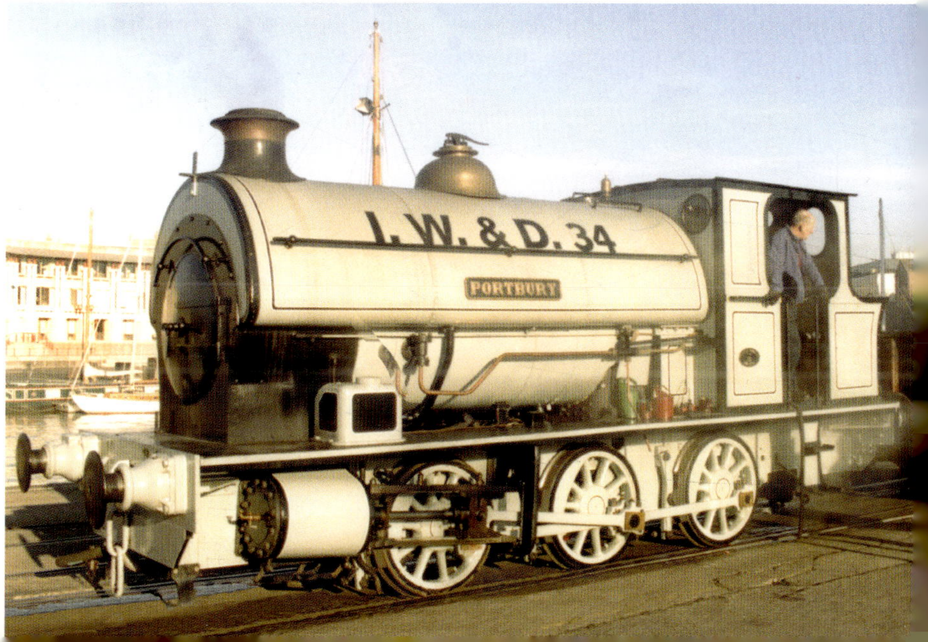

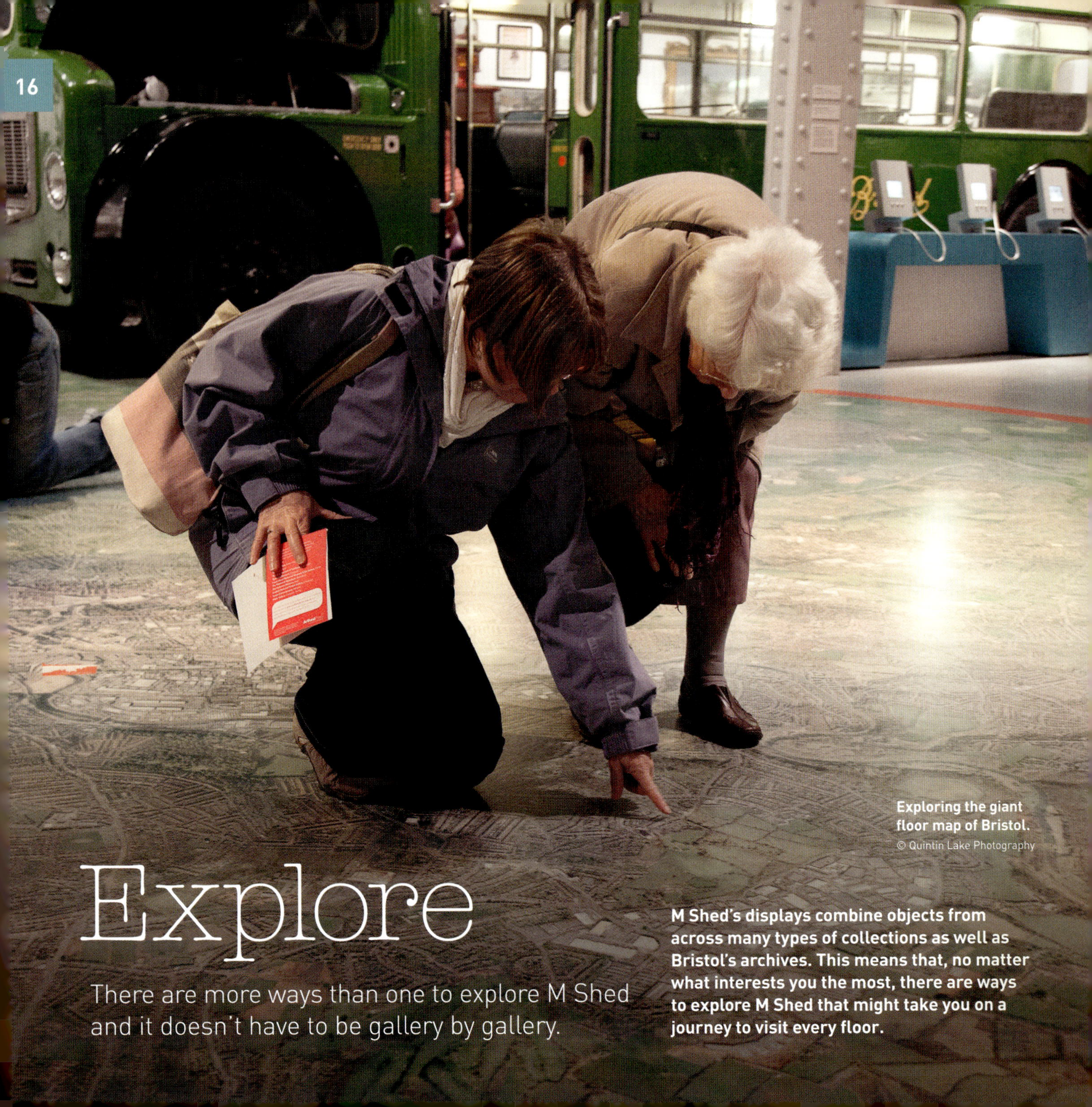

Exploring the giant floor map of Bristol.
© Quintin Lake Photography

Explore

There are more ways than one to explore M Shed and it doesn't have to be gallery by gallery.

M Shed's displays combine objects from across many types of collections as well as Bristol's archives. This means that, no matter what interests you the most, there are ways to explore M Shed that might take you on a journey to visit every floor.

Try…
Digging deeper into Bristol's archaeology

There are over 300 archaeological items on display at M Shed. Here are just a few to look out for although you may spot many more along the way.

Bristol Places Gallery
(Floor 0)

- **Expanding Bristol:** A variety of prehistoric objects, dating from about 200,000 BC to 50 AD. These objects provide us with evidence of some of the earliest human activity in the Bristol area.

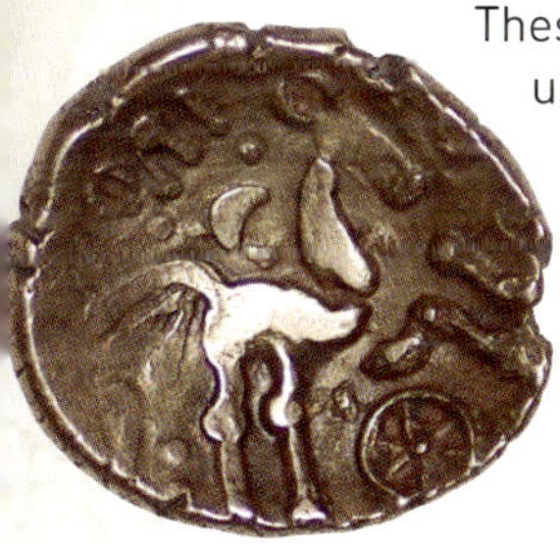

Gold coin of the Dobunni tribe, about 50 BC – 50 AD.

- **Dredging the docks:** A lead ampulla made in the 1200s, as well as other items found in the Floating Harbour. Objects like this were designed to contain 'miracle-working' water given to medieval pilgrims at shrines and holy wells.

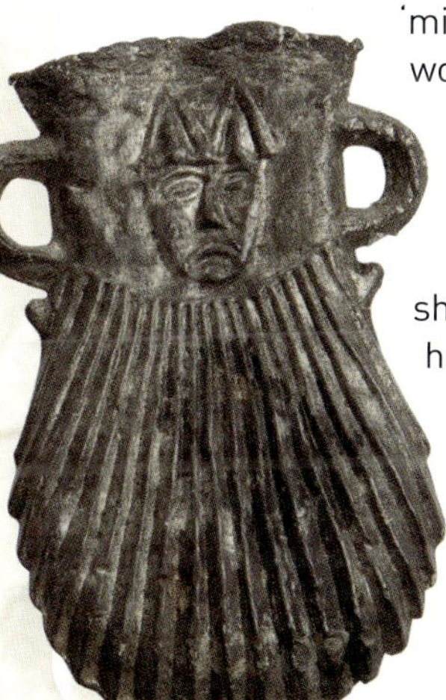

The image on this ampulla may depict St Thomas à Becket.

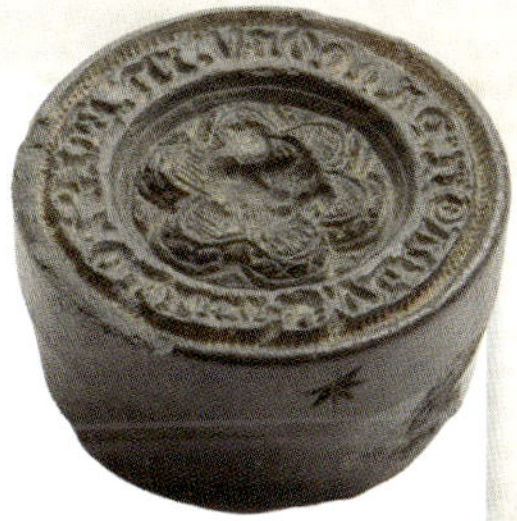

In English the Latin inscription on this seal reads 'seal of alnage of cloths in Bristol'.

Bristol People Gallery
(Floor 01)

- **Trading internationally:** A seal matrix, dating to about 1500, which was used by a city official to stamp his seal of approval on the woollen cloth traded and exported from Bristol in the medieval period.

- **What makes Bristol Bristol, and what Bristol makes:** This puzzle jug was made in the Redcliffe area of Bristol between 1300 - 1350. Ready access to clay, together with local fuel sources such as wood and coal, made Bristol an ideal place for making ceramics.

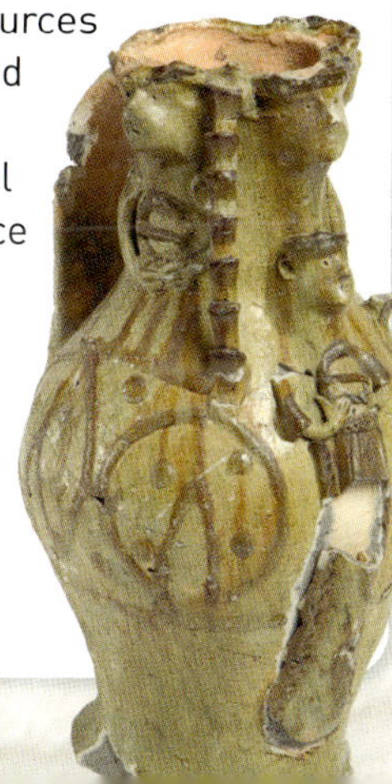

The puzzle is… which spout would the liquid appear from?

Bristol Life Gallery
(Floor 01)

- **Our house:** A pewter flagon dating to the 1300s from the site of a retreat house for the monks of St Augustine's Priory, Bristol. Only one other similar flagon has ever been found in England.

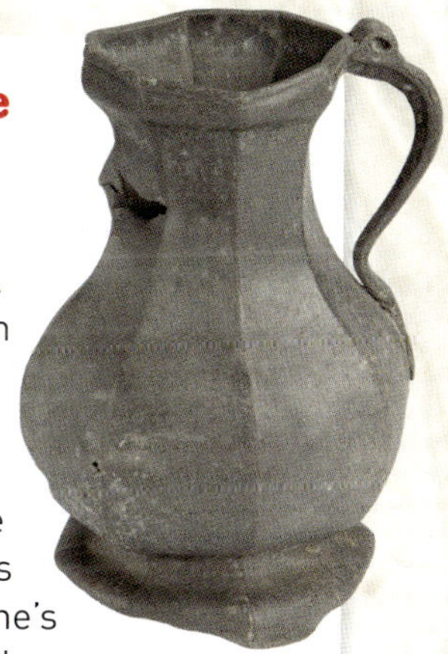

Where this flagon was made is unknown but it was possibly used by the Abbot himself.

- **What do you do together as a family?:** This bone gaming piece was made between the 1100s - 1600s. Counters like this were often used for playing 'tables', which was an early form of backgammon.

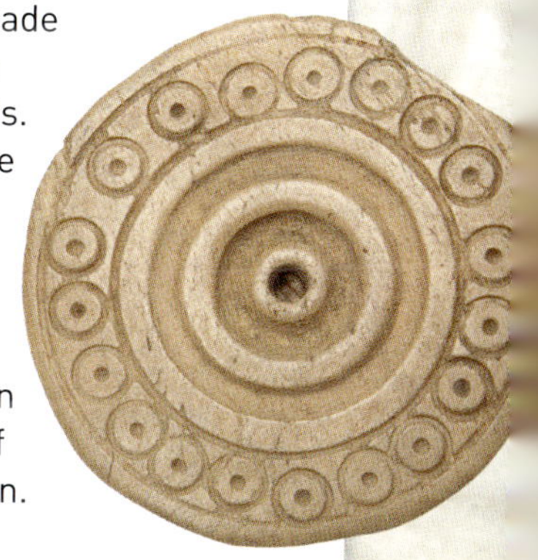

Found during excavations at Peter Street, Bristol in 1975.

Or... Bringing M Shed's artworks into view

If pictures can paint a thousand words then M Shed makes full use of its capacity to tell stories across all the galleries.

Bristol Places Gallery

(Floor 0)

- **Places to live and enjoy:** *The Judgement of Paris*, 1710-1720, believed to have been painted by Pierre Berchet (1659-1720). This fresco was probably created for No.15, Queen's Square, Bristol.

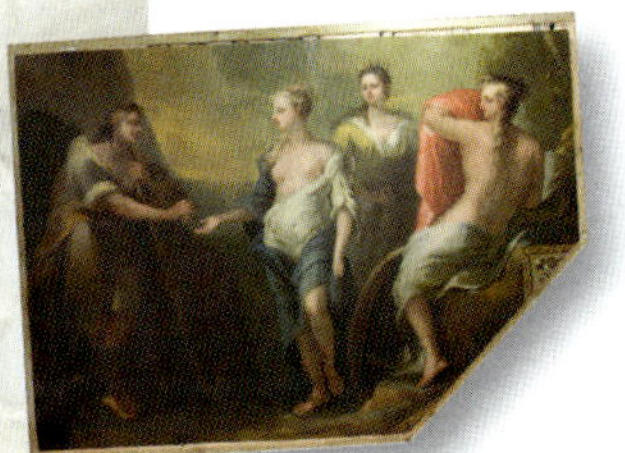

One of several lavish paintings that covered the walls and ceiling of the house.

- **Bristol remodelled:** *Terrace House Demolition, Barton Hill*, about 1963 by Gerald Cains. A record of house clearance in an area considered to be a slum.

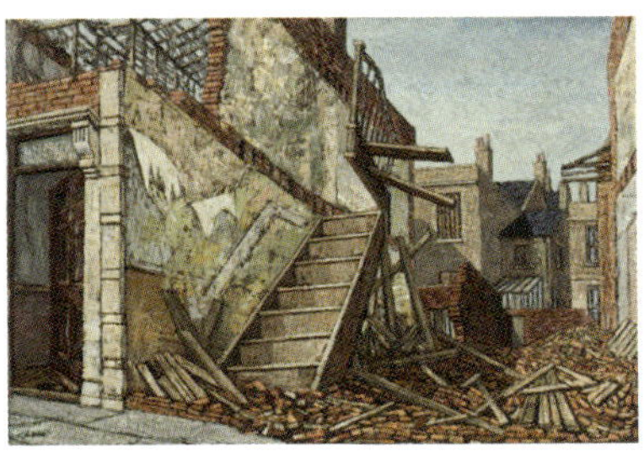

The house being demolished was in Peter's Terrace. Given by the Friends of Bristol Art Gallery, 2010. © Gerald Cains

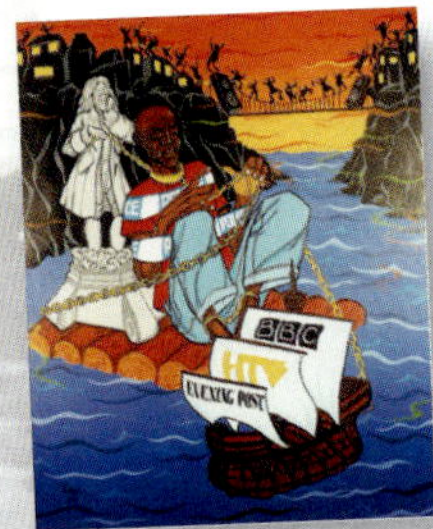

Originally commissioned for the exhibition *'A Respectable Trade? Bristol & Transatlantic Slavery'* at Bristol Museum & Art Gallery in 1999.

© Tony Forbes

Bristol People Gallery

(Floor 01)

- **Bristol and the transatlantic slave trade:** *Sold Down the River*, by Tony Forbes, 1999. At the time it was painted, the artist said of this self-portrait that it portrayed the way he felt he had been treated by authority.

- **What makes Bristol Bristol, and what Bristol makes:** *Fruits of my Life* Lady Gourd by Kate Malone, 2011. This piece was specially commissioned for M Shed and represents stages in the artist's life and career.

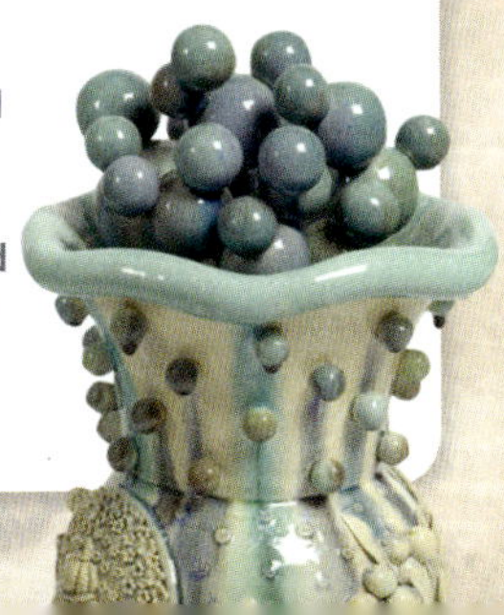

Malone impressed details of where she lived, went to school and studied inside the neck of the pot.

© Kate Malone

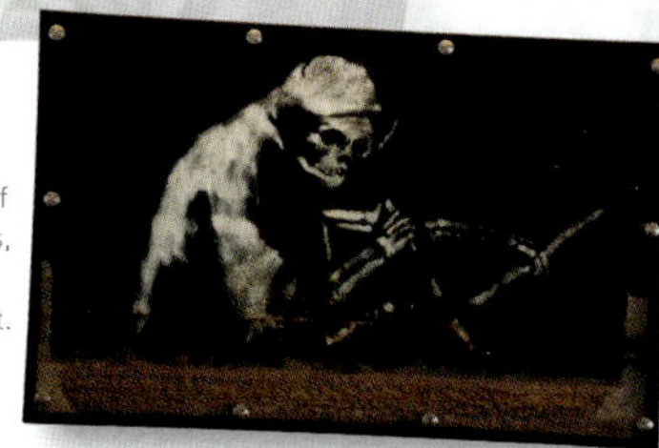

Reproduced here by kind permission of George Akins, DHP Family and the artist. © Banksy

Bristol Life Gallery

(Floor 01)

- **West Foyer entrance:** *Grim Reaper* by Banksy, about 2005. Bristol-born artist Banksy painted this image onto the side of the Thekla, a ship and nightclub venue. Ongoing deterioration of this iconic artwork led to its removal by the Thekla's owners, DHP Family, its conservation and then long-term loan for display at M Shed.

- **Our house:** *Gran Turismo* by Megan J Davies, 2005. Two brothers shown playing the Gran Turismo video game while their grandmother sits beside them deep in thought.

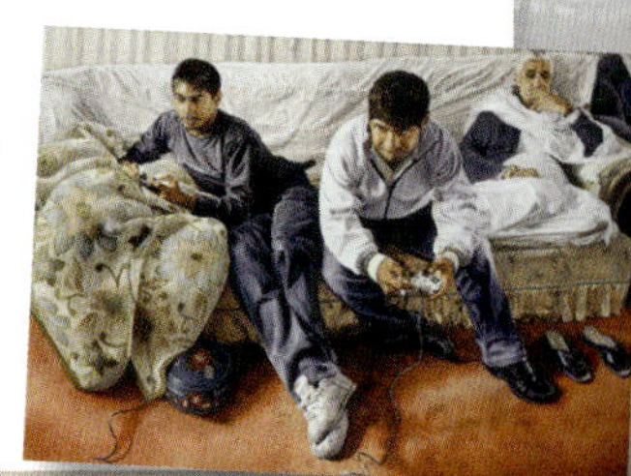

Purchased with the assistance of the Friends of Bristol Art Gallery and the Peter John Blyth Art Fund, 2007. © Megan J Davies

Or... Experience M Shed's sound and vision

M Shed presents its stories in a variety of different ways - search out some of those that are presented as audio-visual experiences across all three galleries.

Bristol Places Gallery
(Floor 0)

- **Moving by boat (audio point):** Listen to John Leonard's and Mrs Fulford's eye-witness accounts of the tragic results of an explosion on the steam launch Red Rover in 1850.

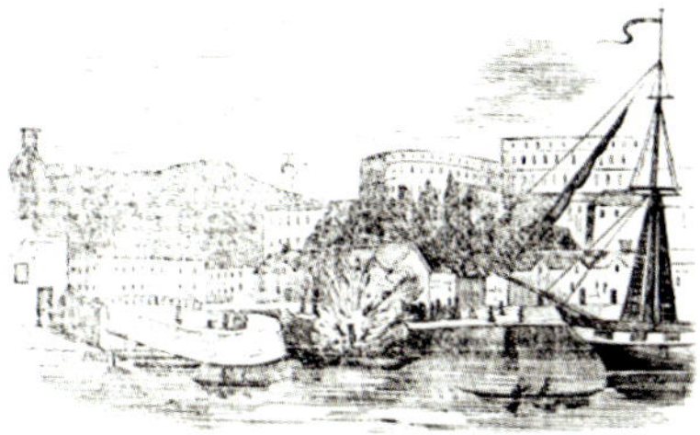

Line drawing that depicts the explosion of the steam launch Red Rover as shown in the Bristol Mercury 27 July 1850.

- **Bristol Blitz:** Watch original film footage of Bristol during World War II and listen to first person accounts of people who experienced the Bristol Blitz.

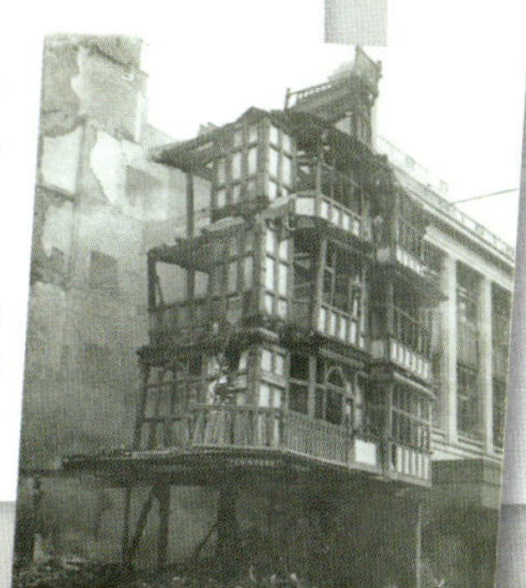

Bristol lost many landmark buildings in World War II air raids, including the Dutch House, which stood on the corner of Wine Street and High Street from 1676. © David Facey: Facey Collection, Bristol Archives 41969/1/67

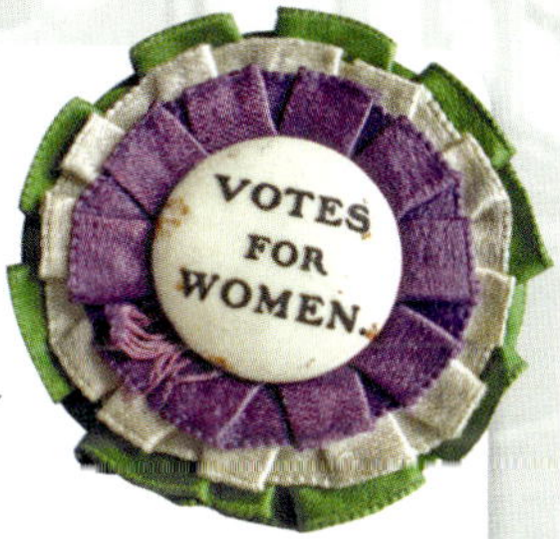

Rosette of the Women's Social and Political Union owned by Ivy Heppell, a WSPU supporter in Bristol.

Bristol People Gallery
(Floor 01)

- **Protesting (touch screen):** Listen to an interview with suffragette Theresa Garnett, who became nationally famous for confronting Winston Churchill at Temple Meads Station over his opposition to votes for women.
- **What makes Bristol Bristol, and what Bristol makes:** Watch a film of handmade glass being produced by Bristol Blue Glass Ltd.

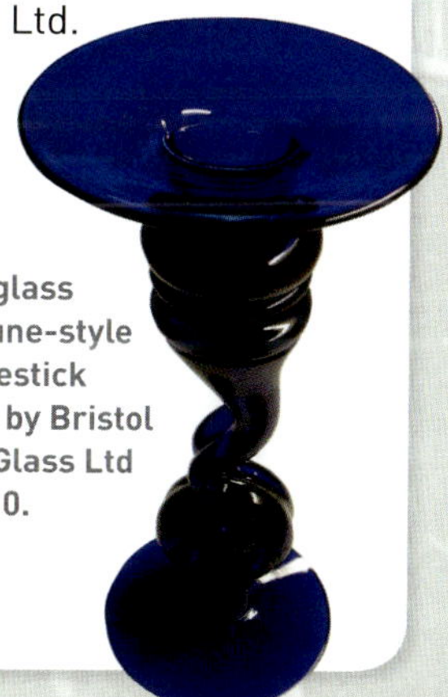

Blue glass Neptune-style candlestick made by Bristol Blue Glass Ltd in 2010.

Bristol Life Gallery
(Floor 01)

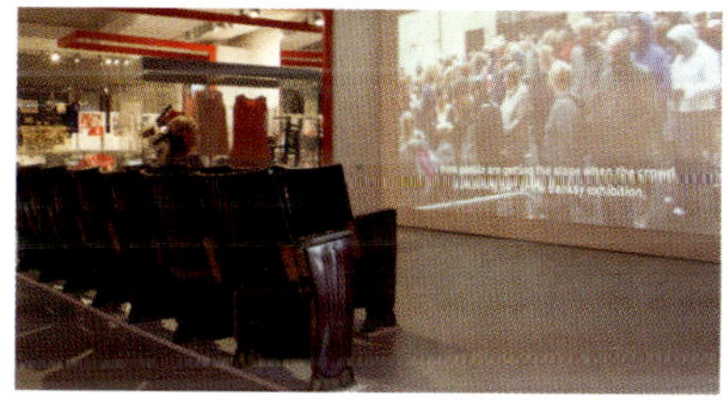

These seats were used by filmgoers until about 1996. © Quintin Lake Photography

- **Bristol with a crowd (movie screen):** Enjoy watching programmed films that reflect life in Bristol while sitting in genuine 1950s cinema seats, which came from the Broadway Cinema in Filwood Broadway, Knowle West.
- **At the gig (touch screen):** Watch an interview with Tony Bullimore, owner of The Bamboo Club, which was filmed for a BBC Points West programme in the 1960s.

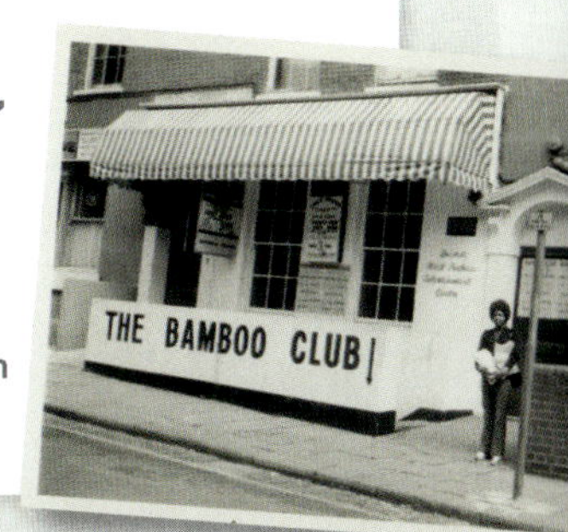

The Bamboo Club, which was set up in 1966, was the first social venue in Bristol to welcome the African-Caribbean community. Bristol Archives 43845/Ph/3/6

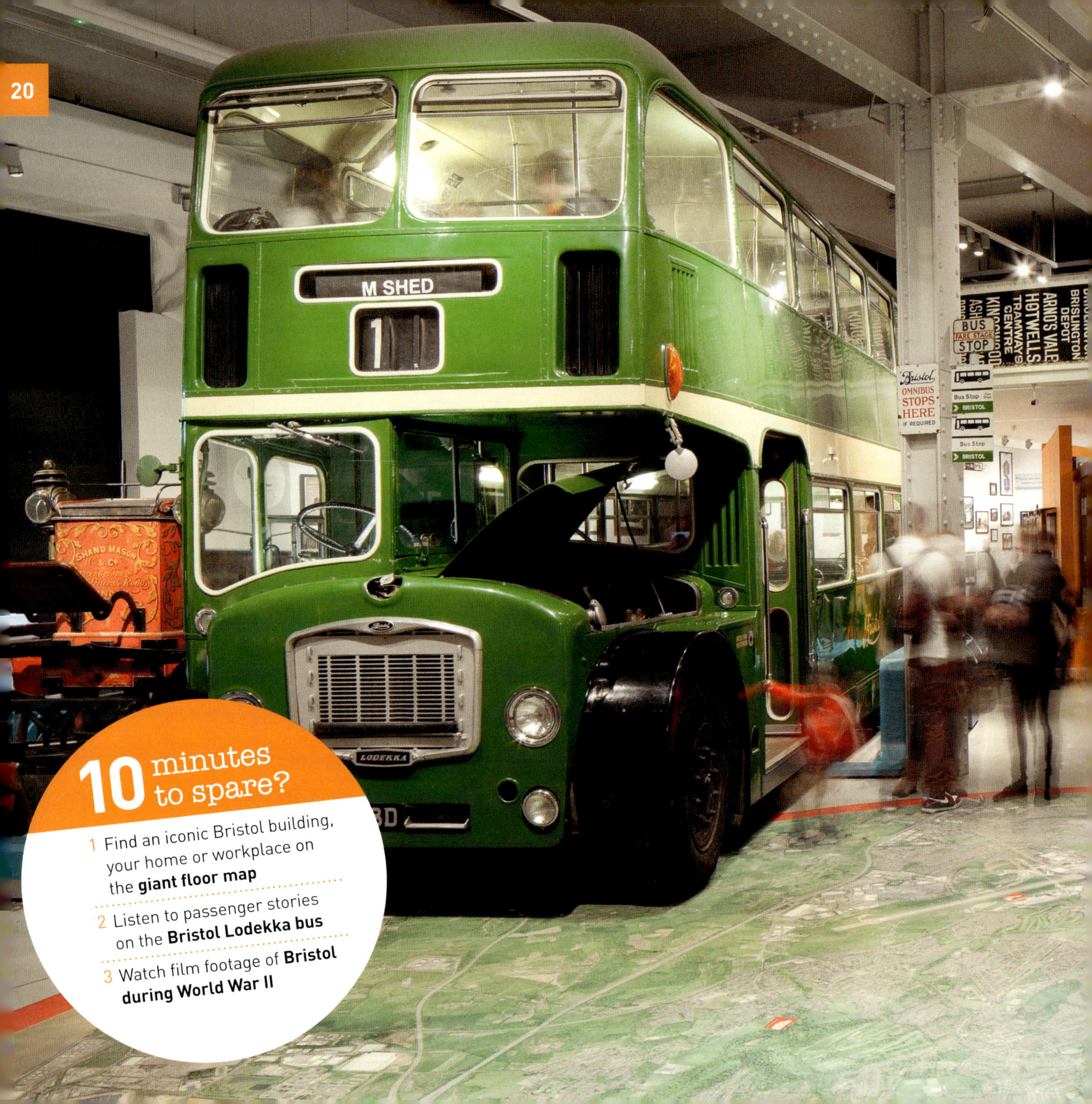

10 minutes to spare?

1 Find an iconic Bristol building, your home or workplace on the **giant floor map**

2 Listen to passenger stories on the **Bristol Lodekka bus**

3 Watch film footage of **Bristol during World War II**

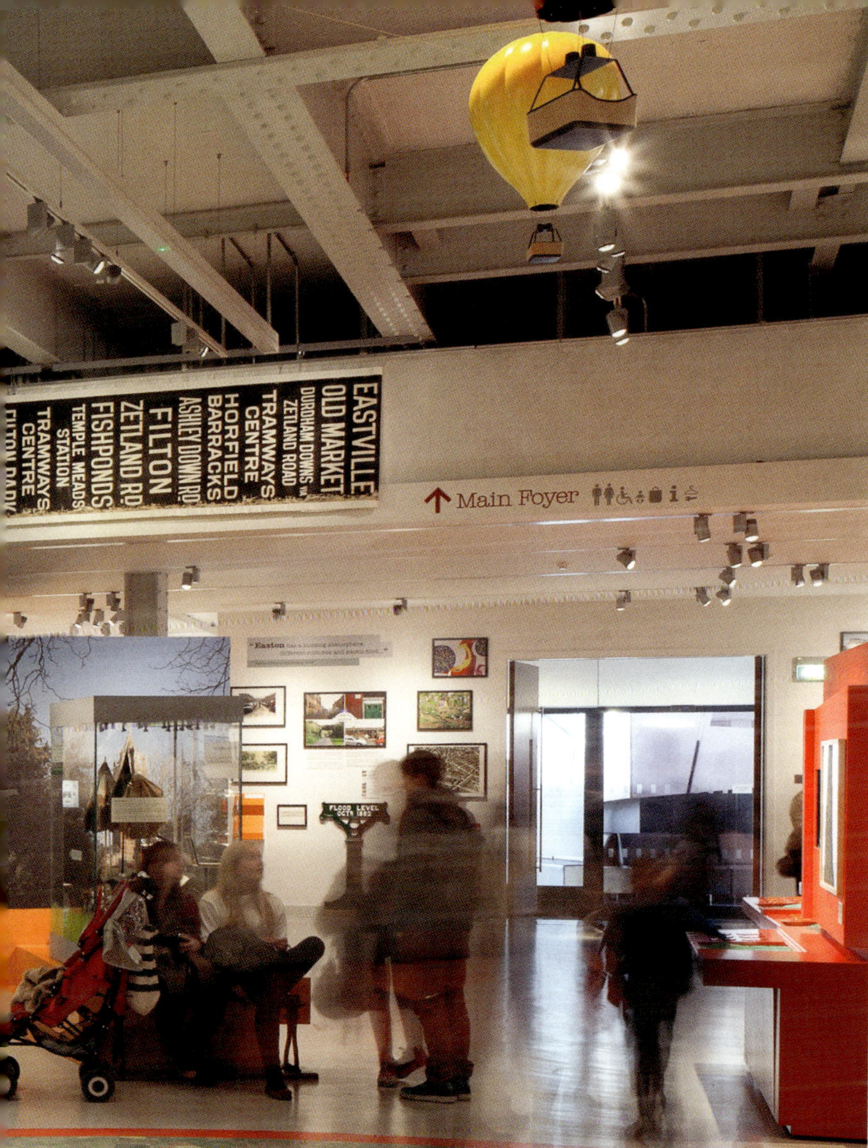

© Quintin Lake Photography

M Shed's galleries at a glance:

Bristol Places

This gallery looks at the ways that people shape and experience the physical city; how and why its buildings, transport systems and other networks have changed over time. It explores themes relating to:

- **Transformation**
- **Movement**
- **Discovery**

Visitors can find out more about:

- **Buildings** – including places to live, learn, work, worship and enjoy
- **Vehicles** – including trams, trains, buses and planes
- **Discoveries** – including dinosaurs, archaeology, nature and treasure

Not to be missed:

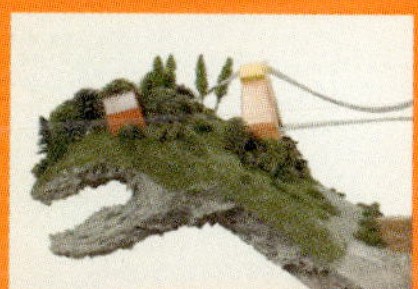

'Brisuanodon' Andy Council & Matt Pugh p25

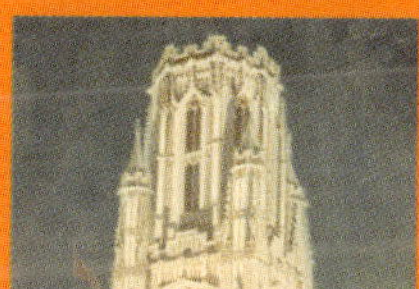

'Coronation Time: The Flood-Lit Tower of Bristol University' Clifford Hanney Cover

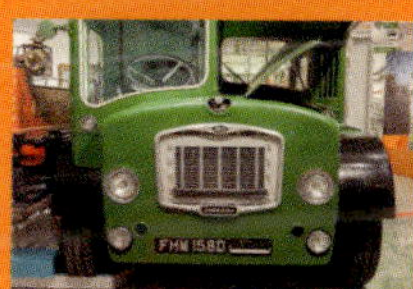

Bristol Lodekka bus p29

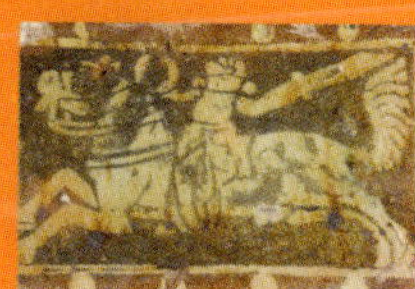

Saladin Tile p28

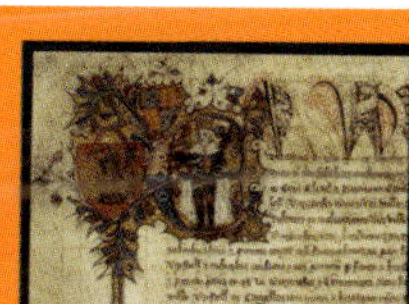

Bristol Charter 1373 p22

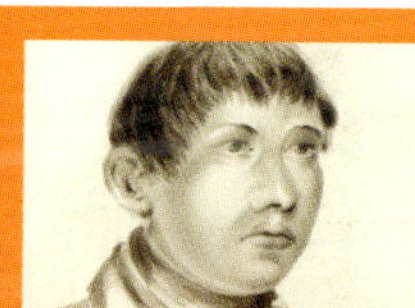

The Horwood Book p28

From Brycgstow to Bristol

Legend has it that the city was founded by an ancient king called Brennius, but in reality it was probably all down to the existence of a bridge.

As far as we know, Bristol or 'Brycgstow', which means 'the place by the bridge', began life as a Saxon settlement that grew up by the lowest secure bridging point of the River Avon just over 1,000 years ago. It was perfectly situated on a well-drained and easily defended spot on a main waterway. This early bridge linked communities and enabled trade just as Bristol's many bridges do today.

The castle and ship that appear on this charter are symbolic of the City of Bristol. They form the centre of its coat of arms and represent its civic identity.

Bristol Archives CC/1/7

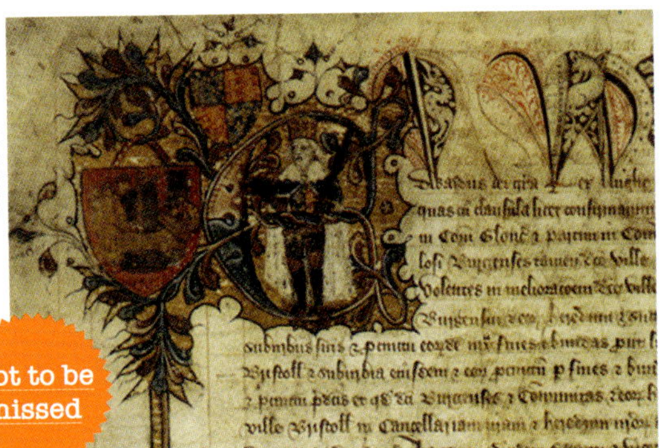

Not to be missed

Royal charters and letters patent: Great Charter of Liberties 1373 (The County Charter).

King Edward III granted a charter to Bristol in 1373 that had far-reaching consequences for Bristol's future governance and identity. The town burgesses wanted Bristol be a county completely separated from Gloucester and Somerset.

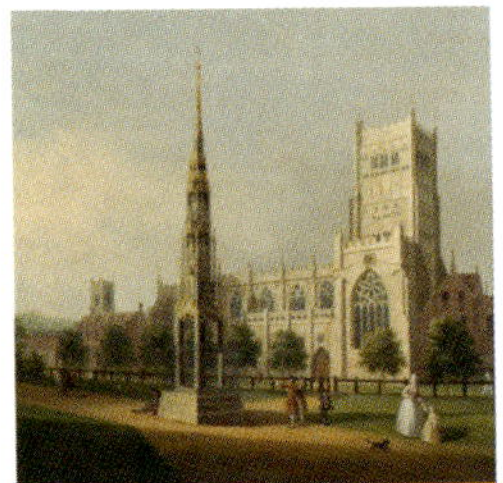

***A View of Bristol High Cross and Cathedral* by Samuel Scott, 1743.**
On display at The Georgian House Museum, Bristol.

Did you know?

The Bristol High Cross is thought to have been erected in 1373 to commemorate Bristol becoming a county in its own right. It was moved to College Green in 1733 after it was deemed to be in the way of traffic. It was moved to Stourhead, Wiltshire, by Henry Hoare in 1765.

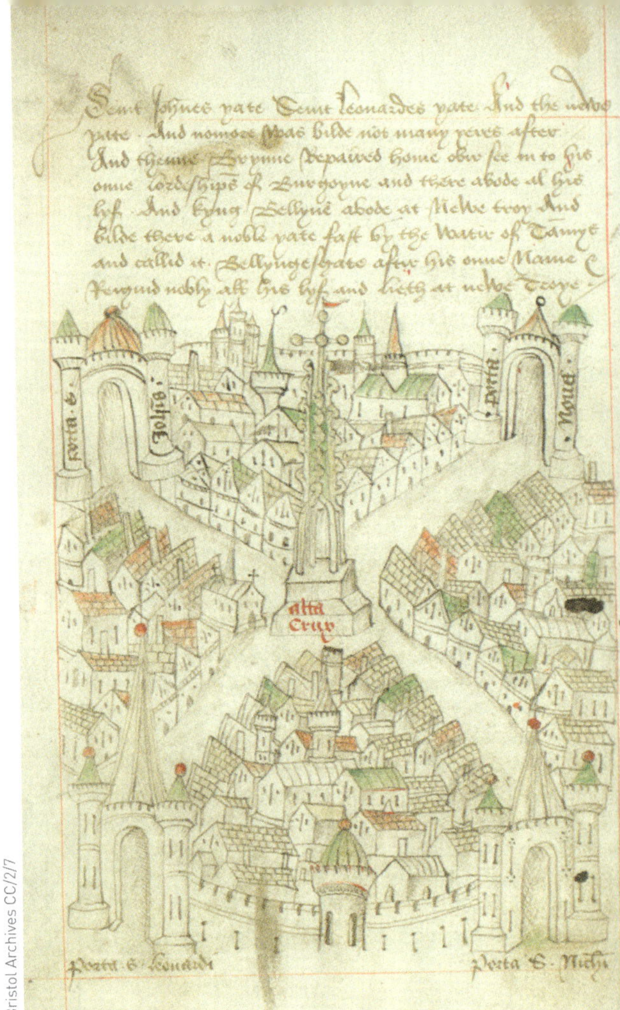

Bristol Archives CC/2/7

The Town Plan, Ricart's Maiores Kalendar, 1480-1508

Ricart's plan of 'Bristollia' is the earliest town plan in England. It shows the town's gates and its four main streets: Wine Street, High Street, Corn Street and Broad Street, all leading to the High Cross.

Until this time Bristol was divided, geographically and administratively, by the River Avon. The parishes to the west and north of the river lay in Gloucestershire, while those to the south were in Somerset. The charter of 1373 made Bristol a county with official powers to make legal decisions and judgements in its own right.

Bristol: a city transformed

People have been transforming Bristol's natural landscape and changing its physical environment for thousands of years, to create places to live, work, rest and play.

They have exploited its natural resources, adapted to local circumstance and sometimes had to respond to national and international events beyond their control. All these actions have left, and continue to leave, their mark as the city's transformation continues.

Places to live and enjoy

Whether it's 'to move up, to move out, or to follow fashion' the reasons why Bristol's people have chosen to develop particular places to meet their needs for homes, entertainment or even just for fresh air can be influenced by any number of factors.

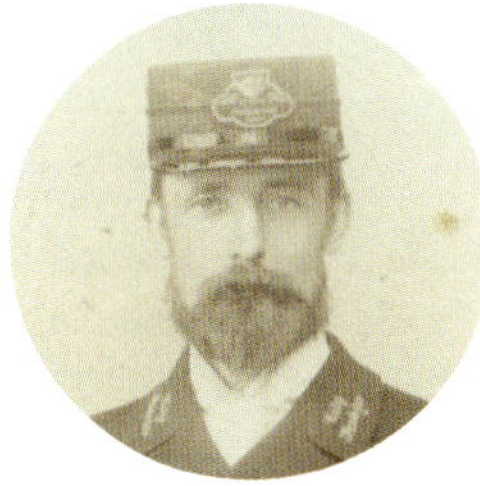

Samuel Edward Cockbill was the City Forester for 40 years. From 1889, he looked after all the trees in the streets and parks, at a time when most of Bristol's parks were being created.

Bristol Archives 37683/2

> **Gallery tip:** *to find out more about how and why Bristol has changed over time, explore the Expanding Bristol display which visually illustrates its continuous expansion using a series of interactive and real maps.*

People need parks

There are now over 450 parks and green spaces to be enjoyed in Bristol but this wasn't always the case. In the 1850s most working-class people did not have access to clean, open spaces so groups campaigned to introduce public parks. Sir John Greville Smyth gifted land to the city in 1881 for just such a purpose. The land became 'The People's Park, Bedminster' and was later renamed 'Greville Smyth Park'.

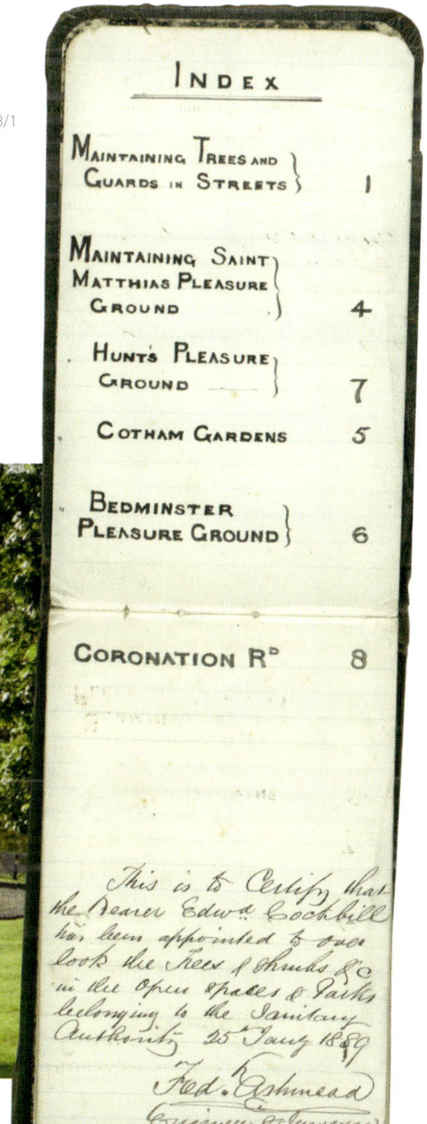

INDEX

Maintaining Trees and Guards in Streets	1
Maintaining Saint Matthias Pleasure Ground	4
Hunt's Pleasure Ground	7
Cotham Gardens	5
Bedminster Pleasure Ground	6
Coronation Rd	8

This is to Certify that the Bearer Edwd Cockbill has been appointed to over look the Trees & Shrubs &c in the Open Spaces & Parks belonging to the Sanitary Authority 25 Jany 1889
Fred. Ashmead
Engineer & Surveyor

Notebook of Samuel Edward Cockbill 1889.

Bristol Archives 37683/1

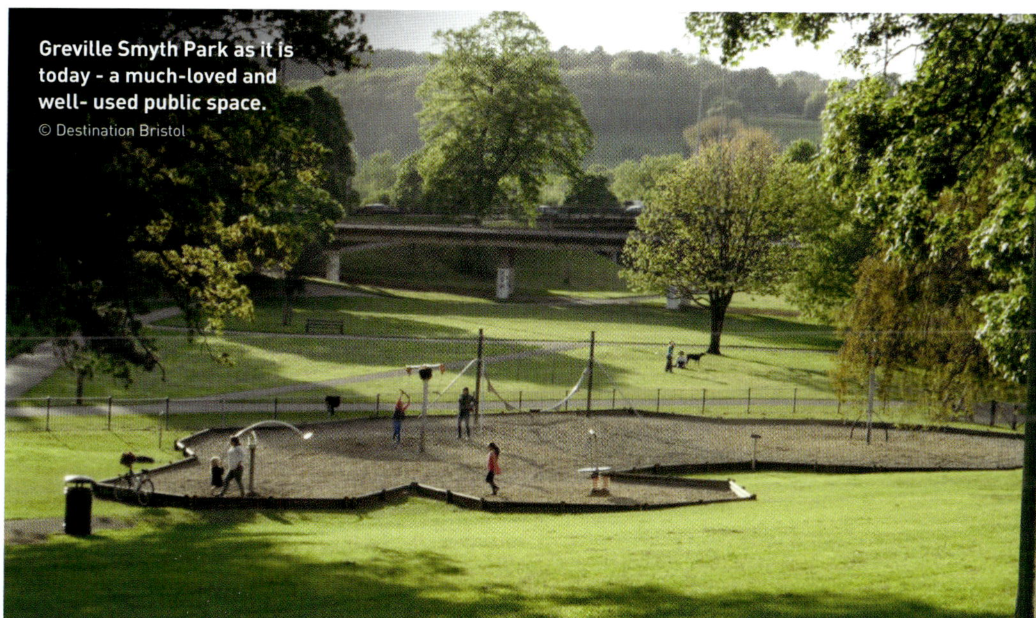

Greville Smyth Park as it is today - a much-loved and well- used public space.

Homes and venues

Alice Chestre's House

In 1472, Bristol draper's widow Alice Chestre contracted carpenter Stephen Morgan to build her a new house in the High Street. Having successfully traded in cloth, wine and other commodities with Europe after her husband died, she clearly had money to upgrade her living arrangements.

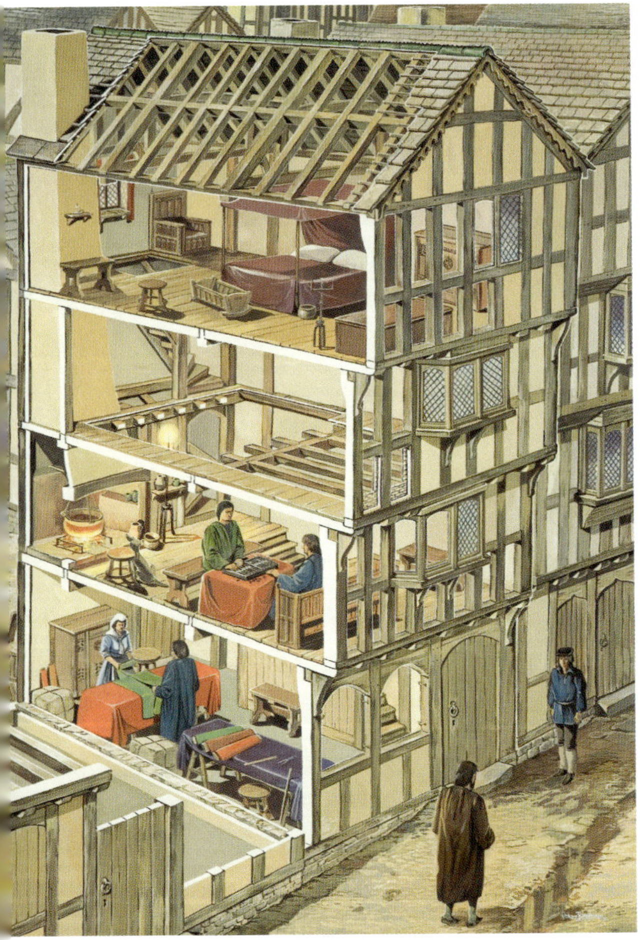

The House that Alice built, 1997, by Graham Bleathman. Most of this artist's impression of Alice's new house was based on archaeological evidence. © Graham Bleathman

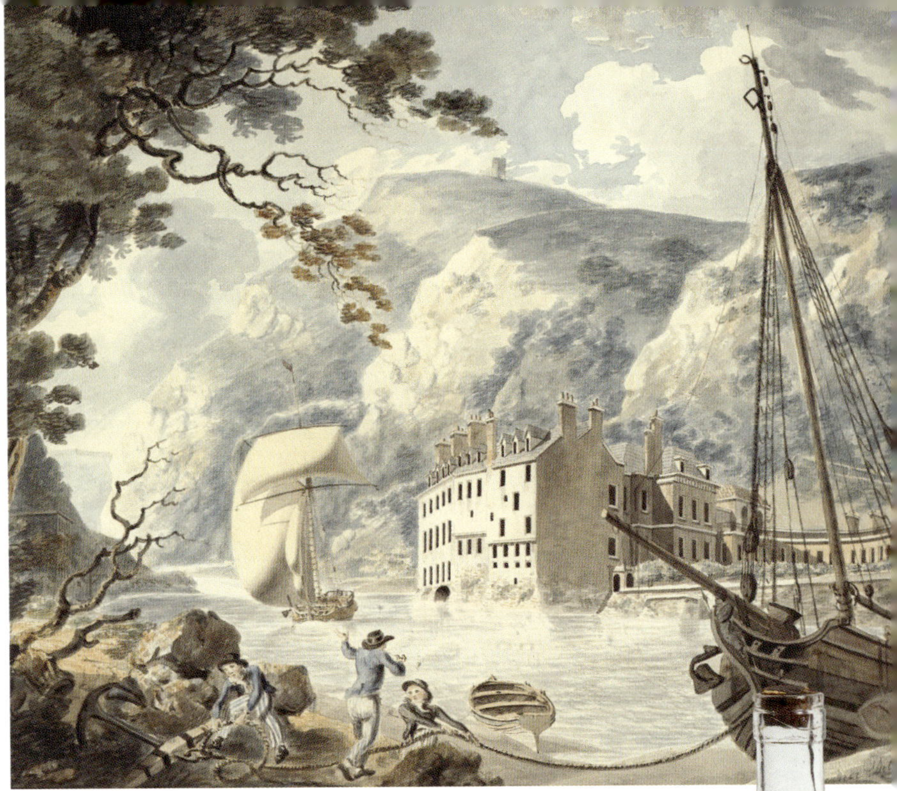

Avon Gorge and Bristol Hotwell, about 1791 by J M W Turner (1775–1851) showing the Hotwells Spa.

Gallery tip: *these stories and objects are just a few of those that feature in the gallery - there are many more to enjoy on the touch screen kiosks.*

At the Hotwells

The popularity of natural hot springs during the 1700s altered the fortunes of a number of British towns and cities, including Bath Spa and Leamington Spa. In Bristol, hotels, lodging houses, pleasure gardens, ballrooms, and shops sprang up to serve visitors to the Hotwells, which became a fashionable gathering place for the rich and famous.

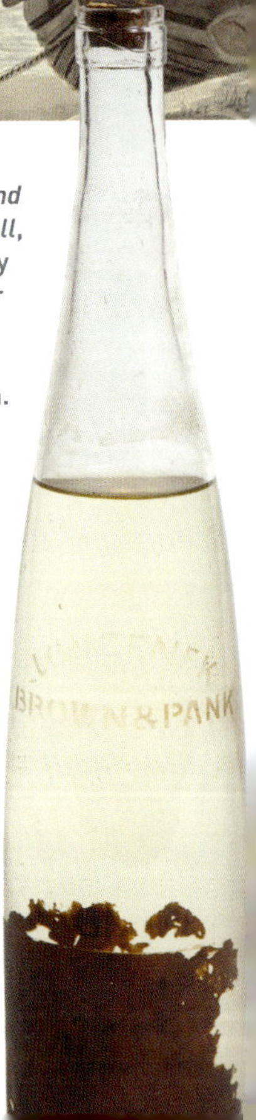

The springs at Hotwells were first recorded in the 1400s when sailors drank from them hoping to cure leprosy. Later, people believed the water's healing powers could cure diseases like consumption (tuberculosis). Bottles of water like this were sold in the streets surrounding the spa.

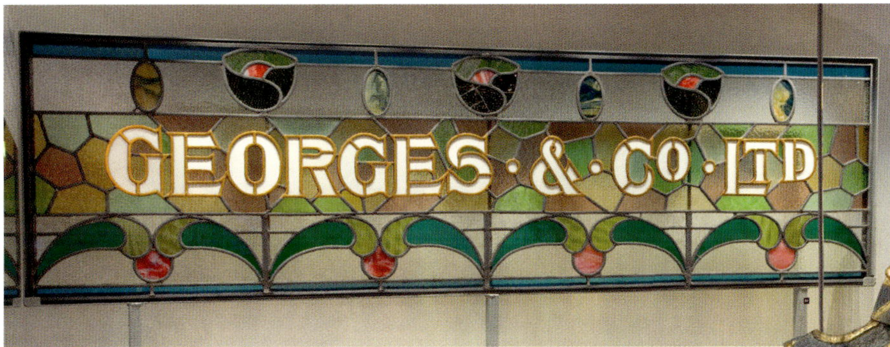

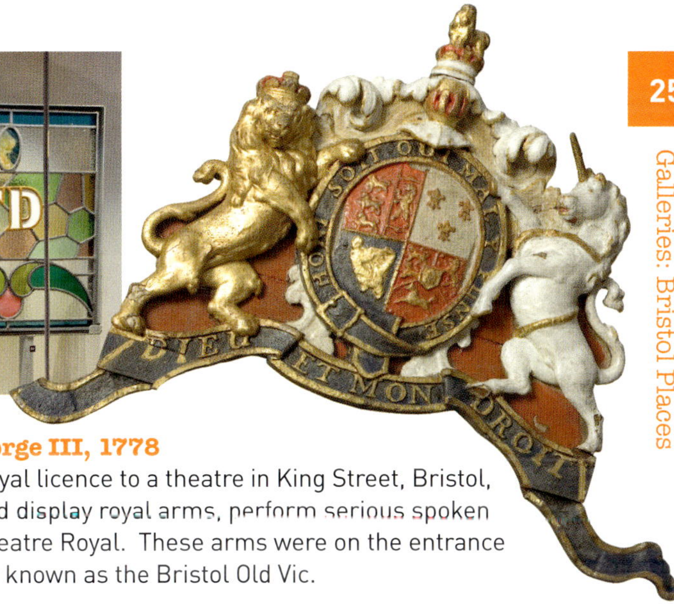

Georges' pub fittings, 1900s
Bristol brewery Georges' & Co delivered beer around the city by dray. The 'greys' (horses) that pulled them became a company symbol.

Coat of arms of King George III, 1778
King George III granted a royal licence to a theatre in King Street, Bristol, in 1778 which meant it could display royal arms, perform serious spoken drama and be called the Theatre Royal. These arms were on the entrance to the theatre, which is now known as the Bristol Old Vic.

Brisuanadon, 2009 by Andy Council and Matt Pugh

Brisuanadon was produced by Andy Council in collaboration with the designer-maker Matt Pugh for the Royal West of England Academy's 'Crimes of Passion' exhibition in 2009. It takes its inspiration from the Clifton Wood and Hotwells areas of Bristol. It is covered with brightly coloured terraced houses and shows Clifton Suspension Bridge crossing over the muddy River Avon.

Bristol's naturally hilly landscape enables views of many areas of the city and rows of colourful properties are now just as much part of Bristol's identity as its iconic landmark buildings, to its residents and visitors alike.

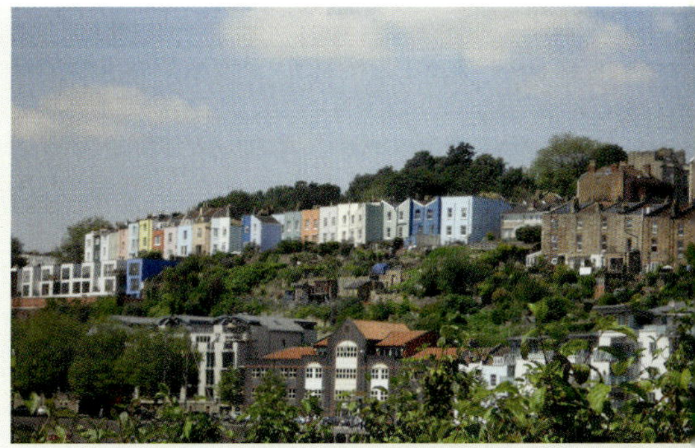

Clifton Wood © Destination Bristol

Not to be missed

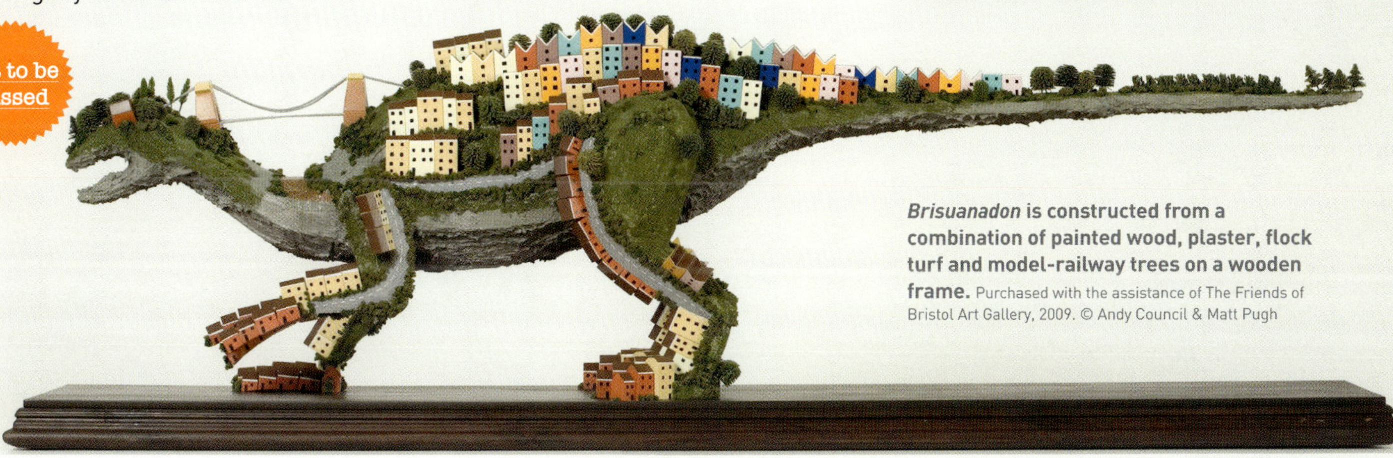

***Brisuanadon* is constructed from a combination of painted wood, plaster, flock turf and model-railway trees on a wooden frame.** Purchased with the assistance of The Friends of Bristol Art Gallery, 2009. © Andy Council & Matt Pugh

Transformed by conflict

For thousands of years Bristol's natural landscape, its hills, rivers and valleys, enabled its people to create both strongholds and places of refuge. Nevertheless, Bristol has been dramatically transformed by all forms of conflict and especially by war.

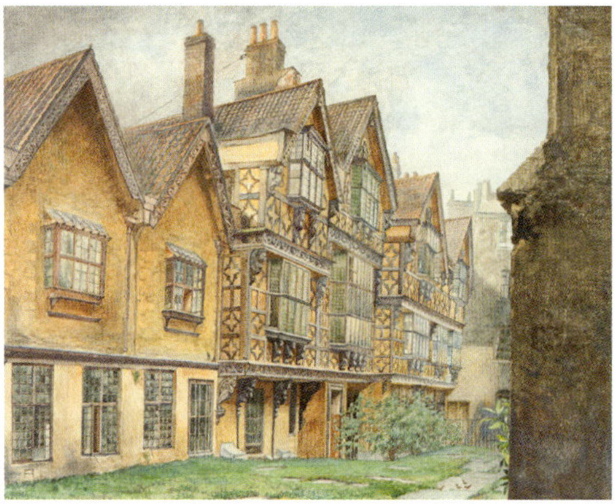

St Peter's Hospital from the churchyard, 1894 by Mary Kathleen Moore (1847-1926). Bristol lost many iconic historic buildings including St Peter's Hospital, which was destroyed during an air raid in 1940.

Bristol Blitzed

Bristol's importance as a port and manufacturing centre made it a natural target for German bombing raids in World War II. The first of six major air raids took place on 24 November 1940, which destroyed homes, historic buildings, churches and much of Bristol's main shopping area. Many of the city's suburbs were also bombed and civilians were regularly caught up in the action. Preparation for war, as well as the consequences of military action, changed the face of the city and people's lives.

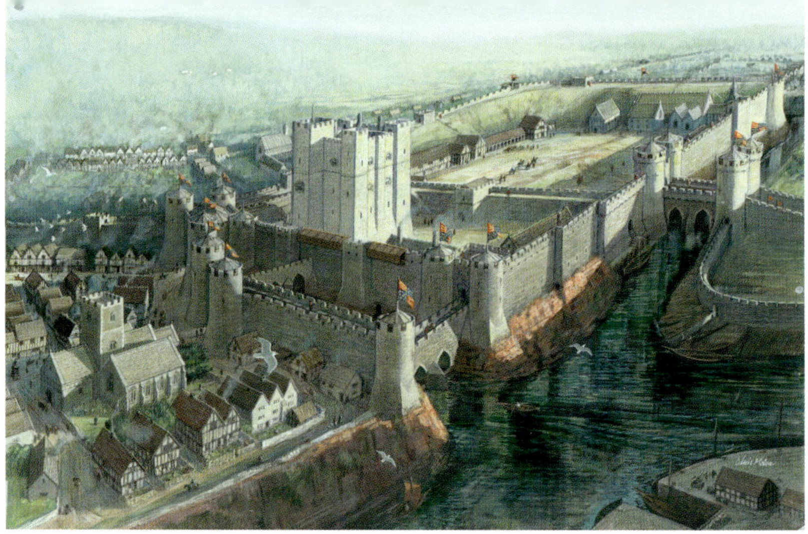

An artist's impression of Bristol Castle by Christine Molan. Parts of the castle can still be seen in and around Castle Park today.

Bristol Castle

Bristol Castle was the most visible and dominant building in Bristol for almost 600 years until it was demolished in 1656. Even though it no longer exists it has had a lasting effect on the shape of the modern city today. The castle was transformed into a substantial building by Robert Earl of Gloucester in the late 1200s. Its massive stone keep and walls were designed to defend it against invasion and to control the town.

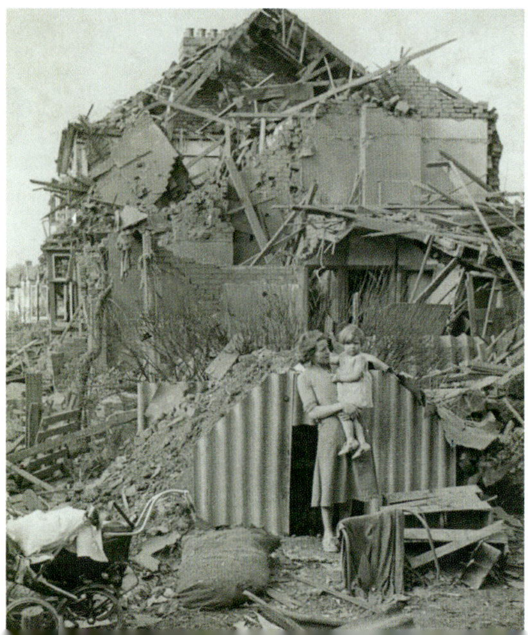

Two lucky occupants emerge unscathed from their Anderson shelter in Filton while all around them is piled the aftermath of a terrifying night. © David Facey: Facey Collection, Bristol Archives 41969/1/80

Gallery tip: *remember to look above the Anderson Shelter and at the gallery ceiling to see more objects relating to this theme.*

Workplaces

Bristol's industries, past and present, have provided it with some of its most distinctive buildings. When one has declined, others have risen to fill its streets and skyline with factories, towers and office blocks. In turn, many of these workplaces have more recently been transformed into homes or for leisure purposes.

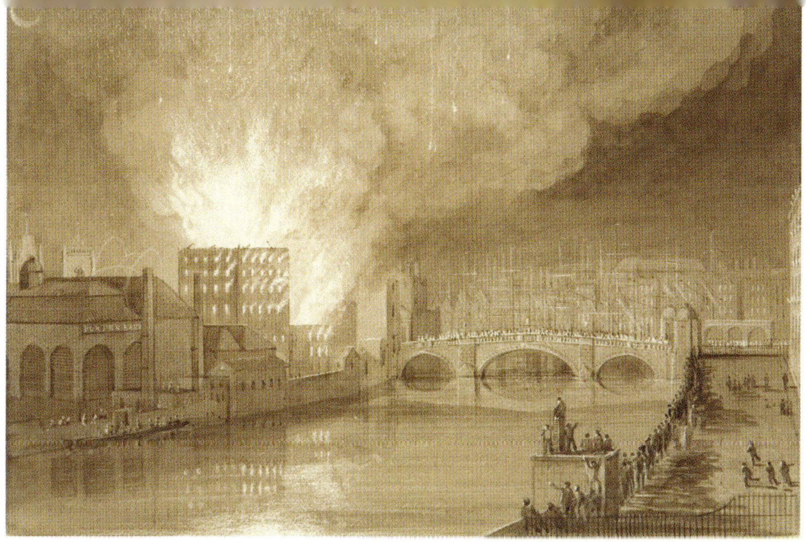

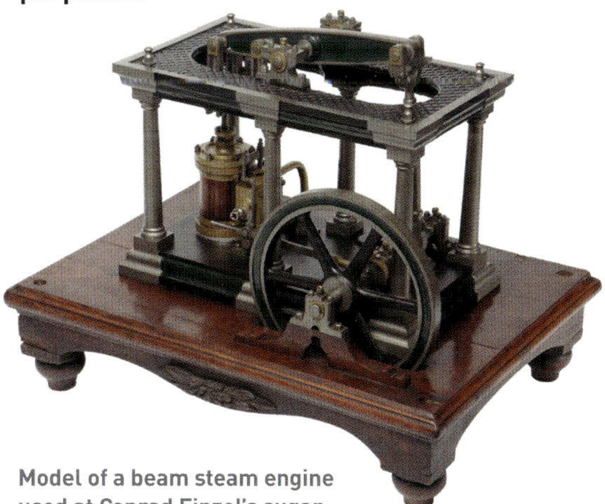

Model of a beam steam engine used at Conrad Finzel's sugar refinery at Counterslip, Bristol. Finzel developed new processing methods that made production faster and less hazardous.

Sugar – ingredient of the city's wealth

Raw sugar was shipped from the Caribbean as a product of the transatlantic slave trade and sugar refining became the city's most lucrative industry. At the height of sugar production in the 1700s, Bristol had 20 refineries that processed about 21,000 tons of raw sugar per year. Its waterways were dominated by six-storey refining houses with tall chimneys belching out smoke.

Fire at the Old Sugar House, Tucker Street, 1826, by Thomas Leeson Rowbotham (1782-1853). Many owners lost their refineries to fire when flames strayed from heavy copper boiling pans.

Wills's East Street Tobacco Factory

A rise in demand for tobacco products and advances in tobacco processing machinery led WD and HO Wills to build a new factory on Bedminster's East Street in the 1880s. It was designed to suit the new machinery, had electric lighting and amenities for the wellbeing of the work force.

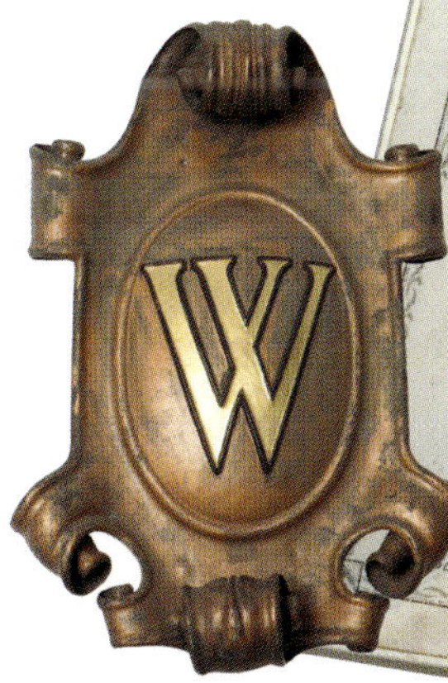

Metal scroll from gates of Wills East St factory.

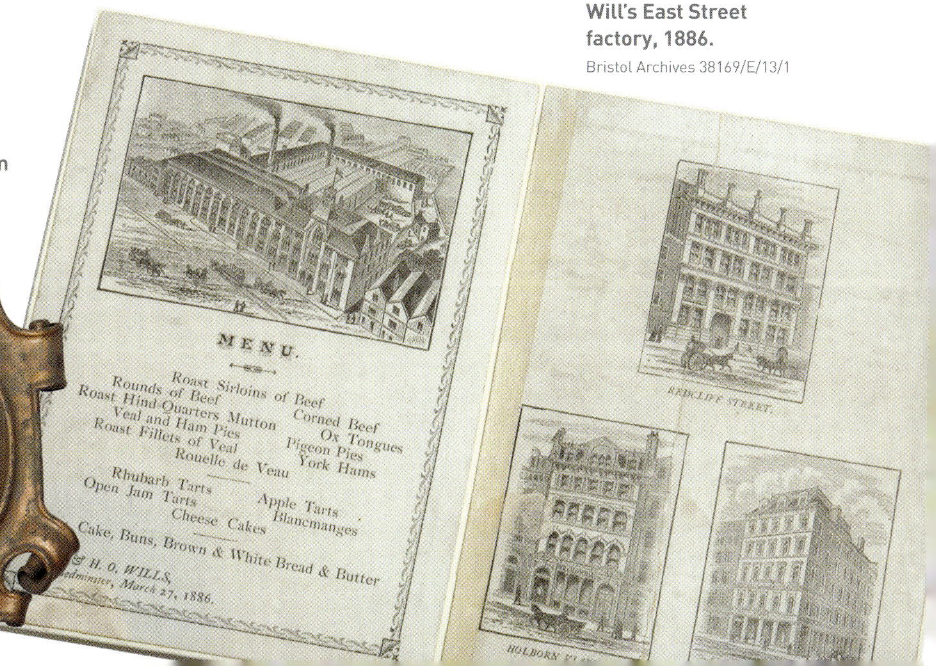

MENU.

Roast Sirloins of Beef
Rounds of Beef — Corned Beef
Roast Hind-Quarters Mutton — Ox Tongues
Veal and Ham Pies — Pigeon Pies
Roast Fillets of Veal — York Hams
Rouelle de Veau

Rhubarb Tarts — Apple Tarts
Open Jam Tarts — Blancmanges
Cheese Cakes

Cake, Buns, Brown & White Bread & Butter

& H. O. WILLS,
edminster, March 27, 1886.

Dinner menu and programme for the opening festivities of Will's East Street factory, 1886.
Bristol Archives 38169/E/13/1

Places of power and influence

Many of Bristol's buildings were constructed to enable people to practice their faith, to provide education and welfare or were built for activities to control or govern their behaviour. Some remain highly visible today but others have been adapted or have disappeared completely.

Not to be missed

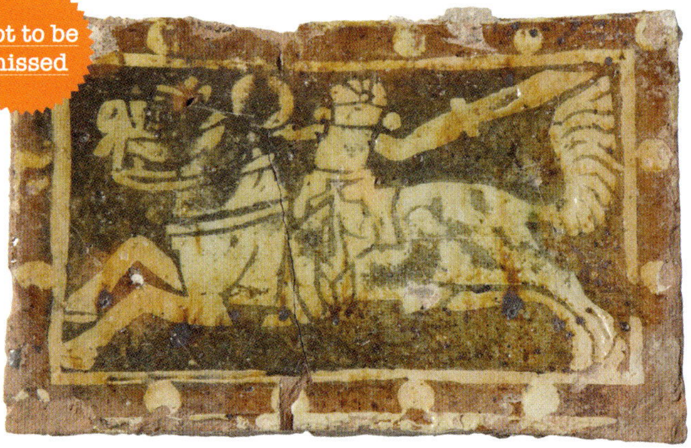

Tiles with similar designs have been found in many medieval religious houses and a Carmelite friary was known to have existed at the Colston House site during the 1200s.

Saladin medieval floor tile, 1200s

This complete medieval tile depicts the Muslim leader, Saladin, and is one of the earliest images relating to the Muslim world found in Bristol. It was discovered during excavations at Colston House in 2007.

The tile is one half of a pair that represented King Richard I (Lionheart) and Saladin facing each other on horseback and wielding a sword. There is no evidence that the two ever met but the story of a duel between them appears in a fictionalised account of Richard's life written in the early 1300s. Medieval writers held Saladin in great esteem as his behaviour matched the highest standards of chivalry. Muslim writers wrote of Richard in return 'never have we had to face a bolder or more subtle opponent'.

Since no photographs exist of John, this sketch contained within the book is the only portrait of him known to exist.

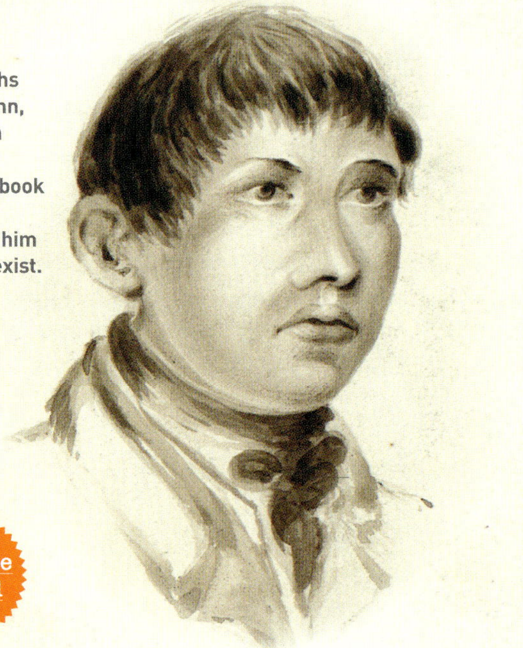

Not to be missed

Book of trial notes: the Horwood Book

On Friday 13 April 1821, Bristol's New Gaol hosted its first public execution. John Horwood, aged 18, was hanged for the murder of Eliza Balsum, an older girl with whom he was infatuated. When Eliza rejected John's advances, he threw a stone that struck her on the head. She died a month later, allegedly as a result of the minor injury to her head that led to an operation on her skull.

During the early 1800s, surgeons were keen to acquire dead bodies for dissection in order to learn about human anatomy. At that time, by law, surgeons could only carry out human dissections on the bodies of executed criminals.

Horwood's body was given to Richard Smith at the Bristol Infirmary for his anatomy class. Smith had Horwood's skin tanned and then had this book detailing the trial and execution bound with it.

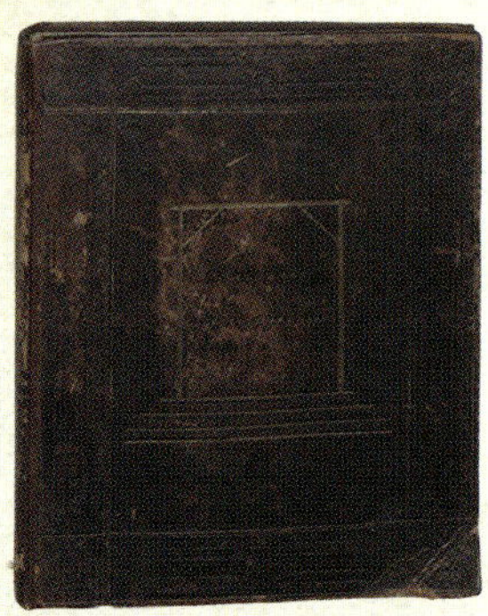

This book bound in human skin is not unique – there may be as many as 47 in libraries around the world.

Bristol Archives 35893/36/v_i

Moving

Whether it is on the ground, in the air, across or on the water, Bristol's people have found many ways of getting themselves, goods and services around the city. From pedal-power to full flight, some may have been more acceptable than others but when it comes to producing iconic vehicles, Bristol has manufactured more than a few.

Not to be missed

Bristol Lodekka Bus, 1966

The Bristol Lodekka bus is the largest single item to be displayed in M Shed and one of the best loved and most fondly remembered of all the vehicles which were on show at the former Bristol Industrial Museum on this site.

The Lodekka was specially designed as a double decker bus capable of passing under bridges as low as 13 feet 6 inches (4.117 metres) and able to carry up to 73 passengers. It was manufactured by Bristol Commercial Vehicles Ltd. and was the company's most successful design, with over 5,200 being built between 1949 and 1968.

Before the Lodekka was designed, most low bridge buses had an offset well in the upper floor and banks of three or four seats situated to one side; this made it difficult for the conductor to collect fares and for passengers to leave window seats. The Bristol design overcame the problem by offsetting the drive shaft from the engine to the rear axle so the lower deck could be installed closer to the ground.

Gallery tip: *stories and information about the vehicles on show in this gallery are provided on audio points – pick up a handset to hear personal experiences and accounts of travellers, drivers and journeys.*

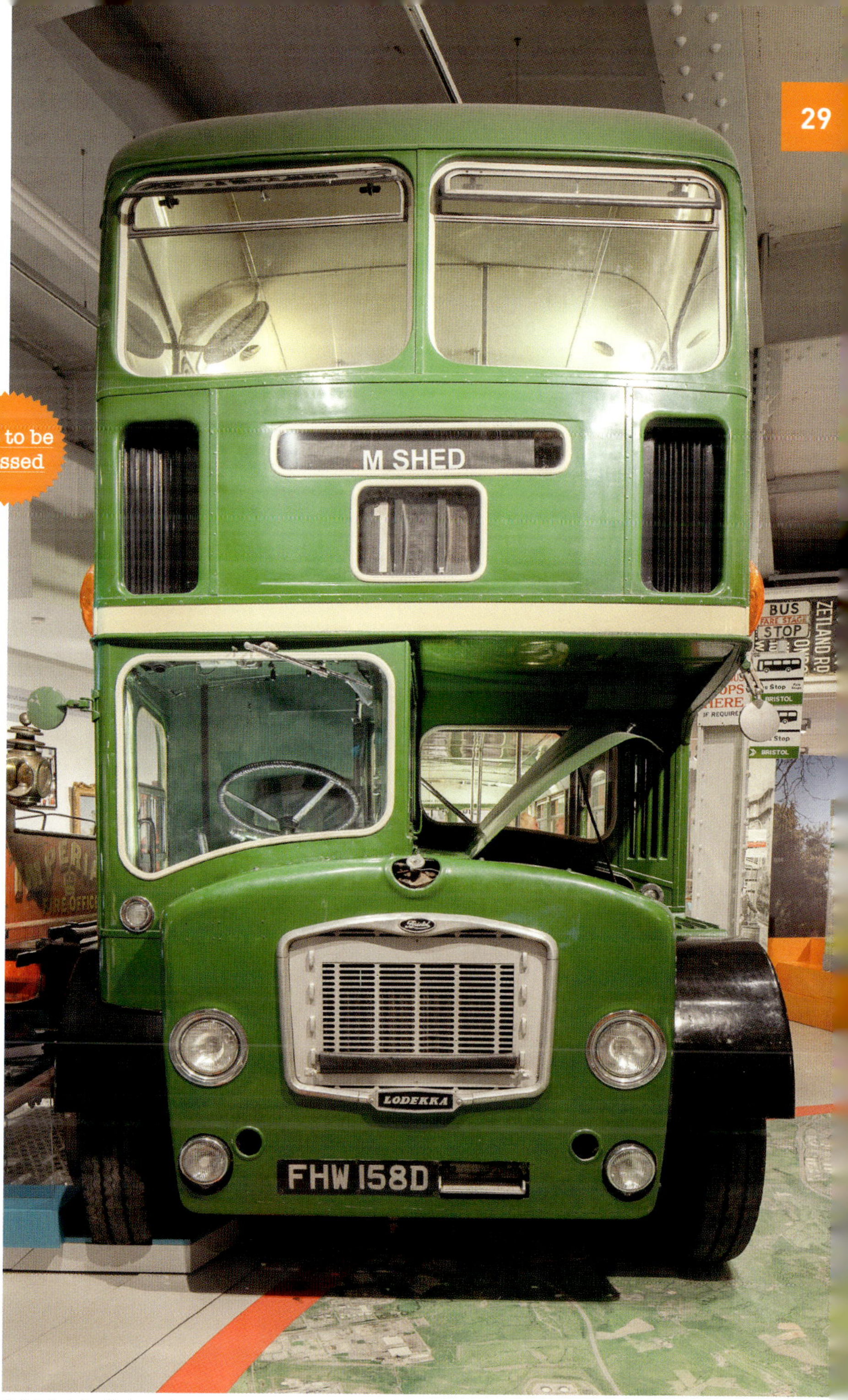

© Quintin Lake Photography

On two wheels...

Francis Fry's record-setting ride

Although cycling was all the rage at the end of the 1800s, as a sport it was mainly the preserve of wealthy young men such as record-breaking Bristolian Francis Fry. Francis was a member of the famous chocolate-making family, J S Fry & Sons, and a member of the Clifton Bicycle Club. He set the record for riding 100 miles on a solid-tyred bicycle in just under six hours in 1883. The record is believed to stand to this day.

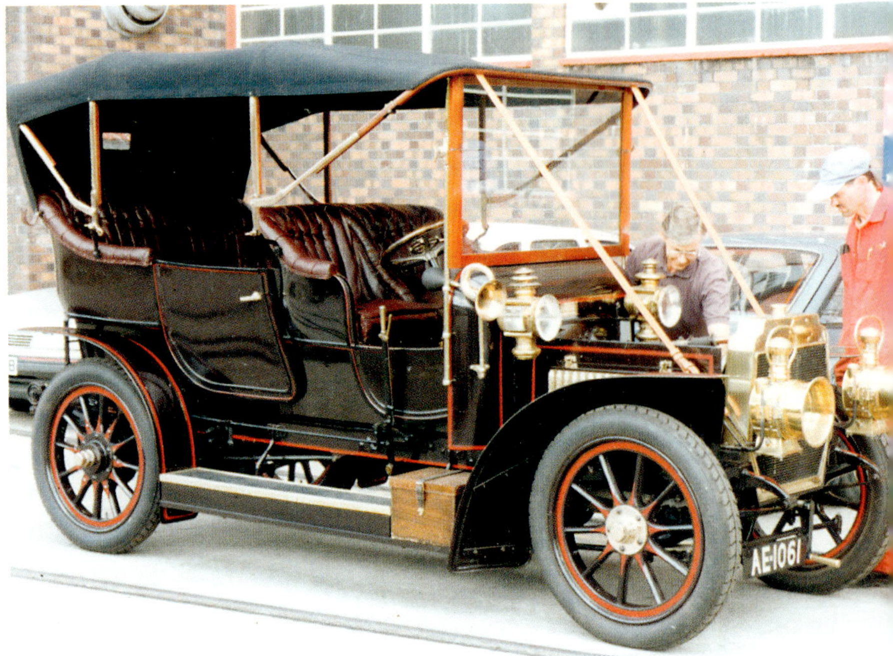

The Colonel's Bristol 16/20 horsepower Type T Tourer fully restored.

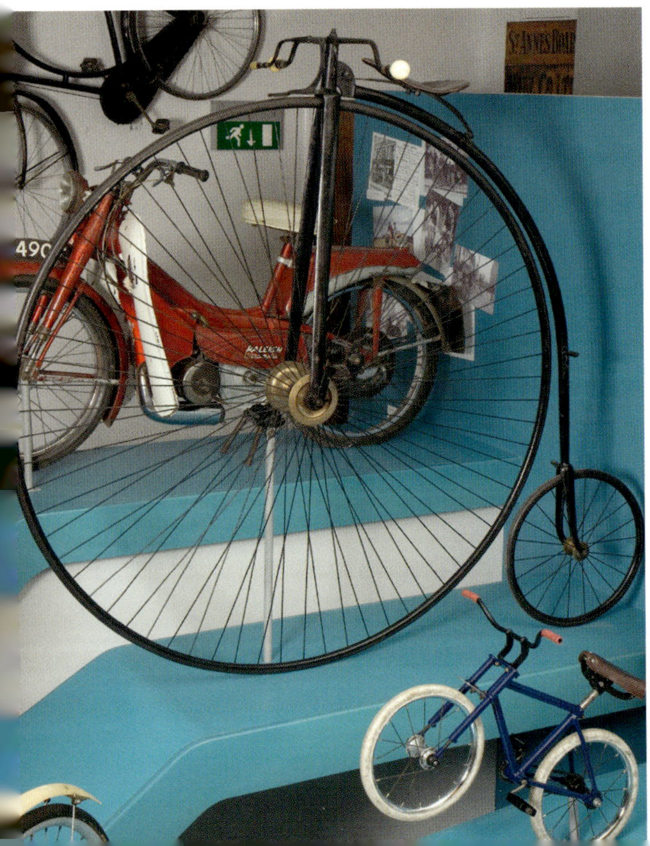

Francis Fry's 'Clifton' bicycle which was made for him by Thomas Pitcher of Lewin's Mead, Bristol.

...and then on four...

The Colonel's Car

Colonel Rolleston's car was delivered by the Bristol Motor Company in 1906 and was similar in some respects to the horse-drawn carriage it replaced. Its body was custom-made by coachbuilders to the Colonel's design, but instead of being driven by a coachman, it was driven by a chauffeur. Rendered obsolete by advances in car manufacture, and with its back seat removed, it was used first as a pick-up truck and then to power a saw bench. It was donated to the museum in 1938.

Did you know?

Bristol Bicycle & Motor Club

Bristol Bicycle Club was one of the earliest cycling clubs in the UK. It was formed in 1876, just seven years after the modern bicycle had been invented. Members organised regular race and time trial meetings. By 1907, the Bristol Bicycle Club had become the Bristol Bicycle & Motor Club, reflecting the growing interest in motorcycles and cars.

...as well as up in the air!

From hot air balloons to skateboards, people in Bristol have experimented and continue to embrace unusual ways of getting around the city, with varying degrees of success. Many of these involved flying in the form of one aircraft or another and some conjectured that 'when motor cars fly. Bristol will build them.'

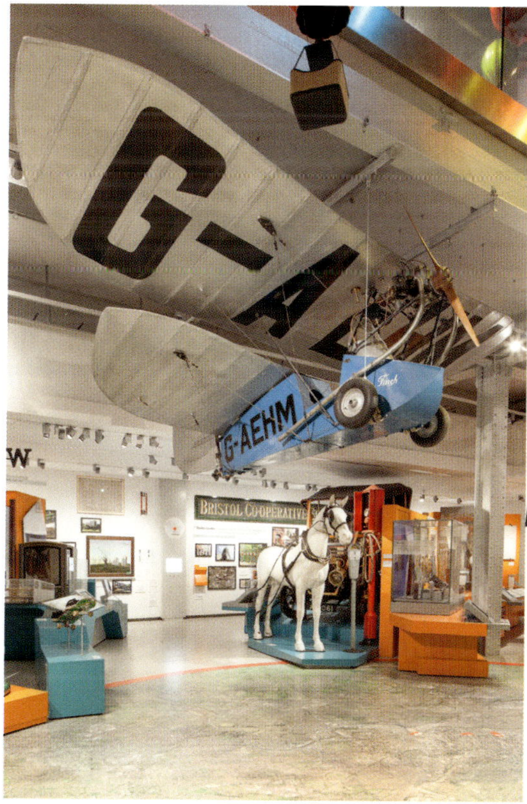

The 'Flying Flea' is on loan to M Shed from the Science Museum, Wroughton.

© Quintin Lake Photography

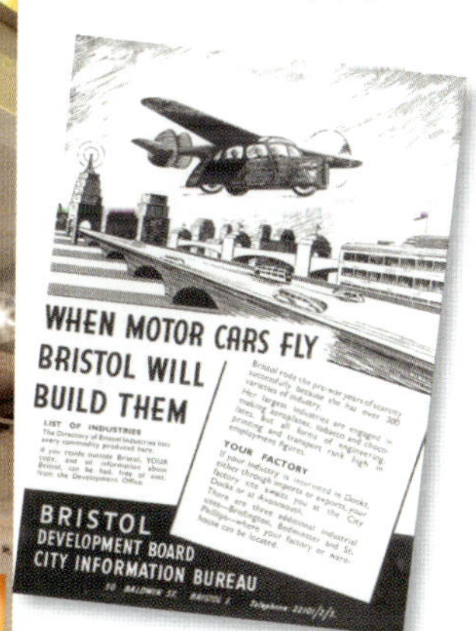

Promotional advert for Bristol factory sites "When Motor Cars Fly, Bristol Will Build Them" by Bristol Development Board. Published in the 1948 PBA Handbook.

'Flying Flea' – kit plane for amateurs, 1930s

Flying literally started to take off in the 1920s and 1930s. Henri Mignet's *Pou De Ciel* (Flying Flea) was a kit-based aircraft that could be built by amateurs. In 1936, Harry Dolman, a Bristol engineer and businessman, was the first to build a Flying Flea in England. He called his the Blue Finch. Its first flight was from Whitchurch Airport, Bristol, when it managed to travel 50 yards (46 metres), reaching a height of 20 feet (six metres) before hitting the ground where it overturned. Luckily Harry was unscathed but he was banned from flying there again.

1:24 scale model of the Bristol Biplane (Boxkite) aircraft, 1910

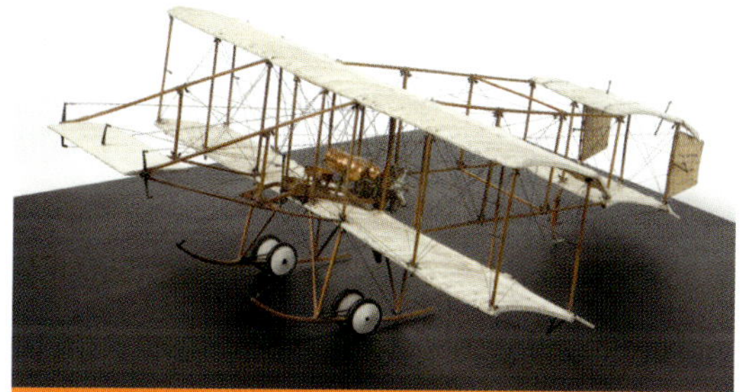

Did you know?

The Bristol biplane (known as a Boxkite) was the first Bristol-manufactured aircraft produced by businessman and transport pioneer, Sir George White, from 1910. The very first Boxkite made three short test flights on 11 November 1910, in heavy rain on Durdham Downs, Bristol.

And finally...

Gallery tip: *don't forget to look out for stories of amazing discoveries that have been made in and around Bristol: they are located at the end of each of the plinths. There are five to find:*

- **The Bristol Dinosaur** – a 'socket-toothed lizard of antiquity'.
- **The Welsh Back Coin Hoard** - treasure beneath the floor.
- **The Conservator's story** – rediscovering the Queen's Square fresco.
- **Our Roman Roots** – the discovery of Kings Weston Roman Villa.
- **Dredging up the docks** – revealing Bristol's connections with pilgrimage.

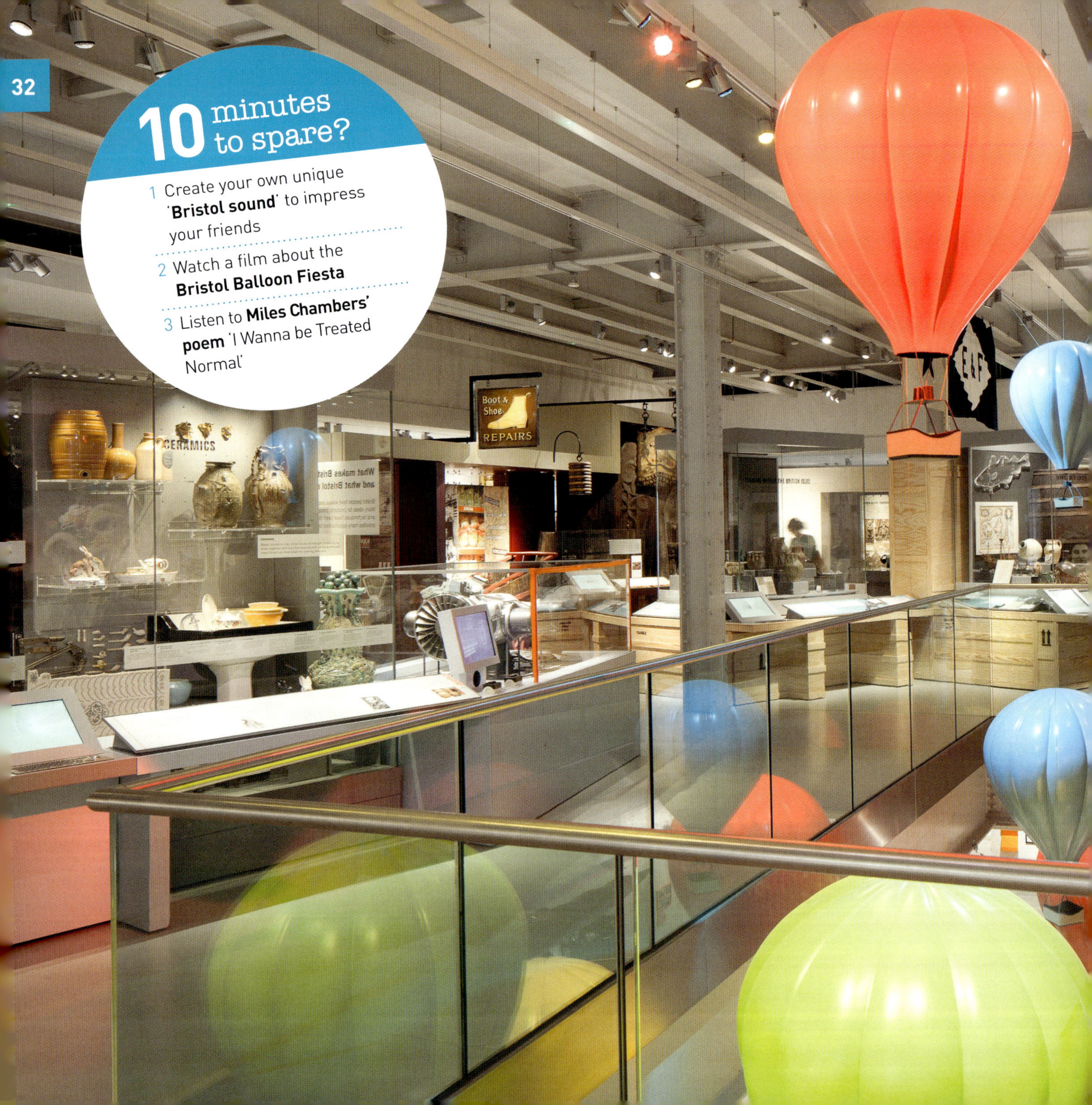

10 minutes to spare?

1 Create your own unique '**Bristol sound**' to impress your friends

2 Watch a film about the **Bristol Balloon Fiesta**

3 Listen to **Miles Chambers' poem** 'I Wanna be Treated Normal'

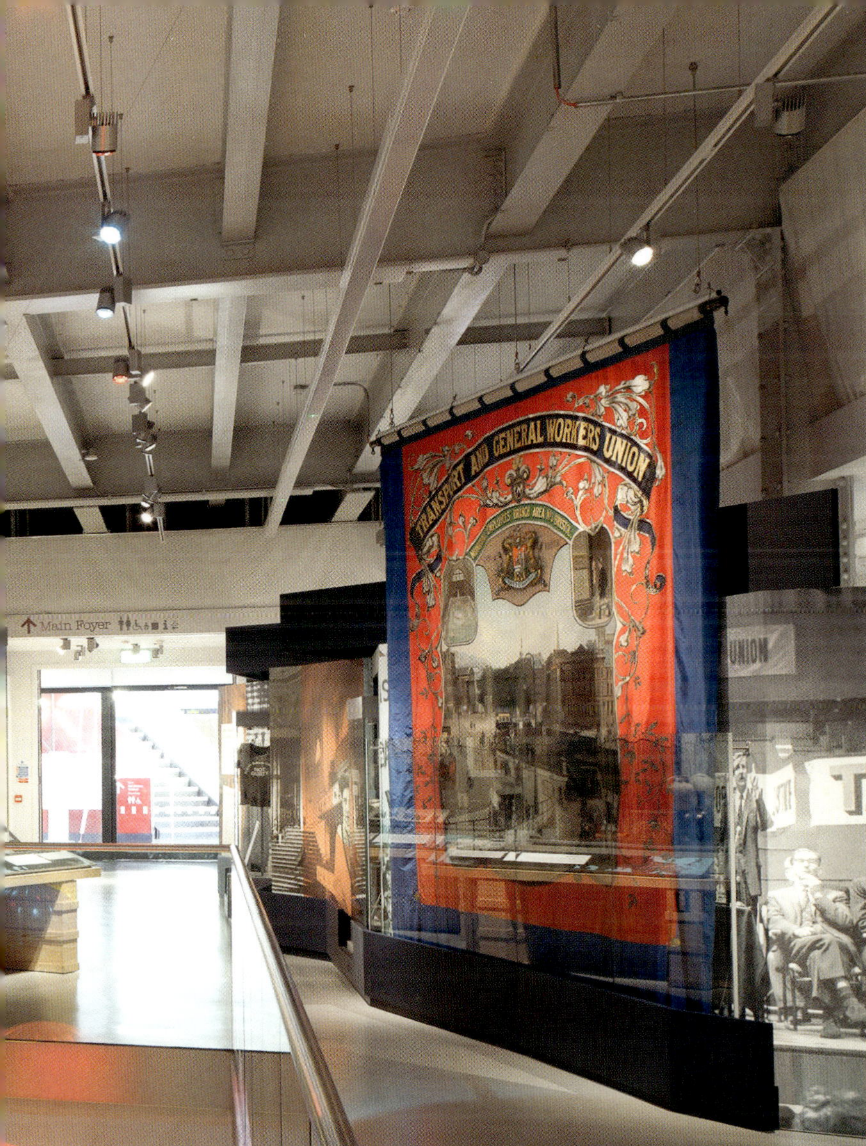

© Quintin Lake Photography

M Shed's galleries at a glance:

Bristol People

This gallery explores the ways in which people have shaped, and continue to shape, the fortunes of the city and how their activities, from music and art to industry, technology and philanthropy, define its character. It explores themes relating to:

- **Trading**
- **Celebrating**
- **Creating**
- **Challenging**

Visitors can find out more about:

- Trade and exchange
- The Transatlantic Slave Trade and its legacy
- Local festivals, ceremonies and processions
- Bristolian creativity, ingenuity and artistry
- Responses to injustice: riots, protests and reform

Not to be missed:

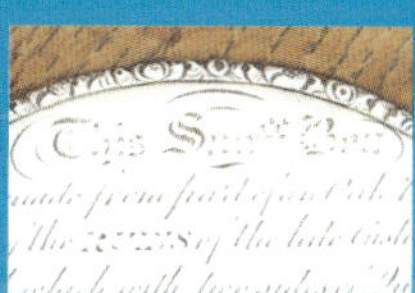

Souvenirs of the 1831 Reform Riots **p39**

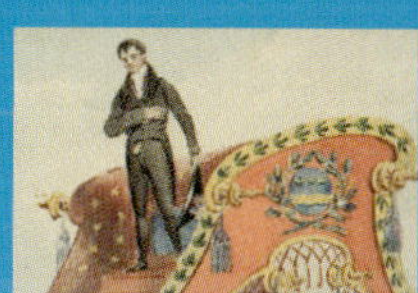

***The Chairing of Henry Bright* panorama** **p42**

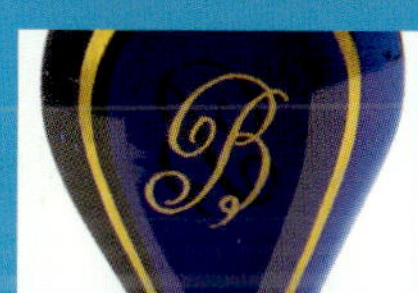

Bristol Blue Glass **p40**

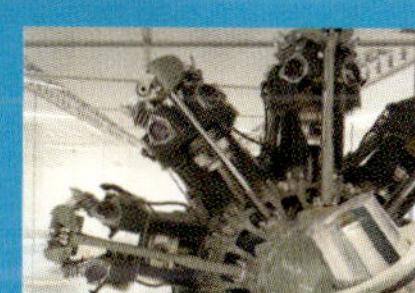

Bristol Pegasus radial engine **p41**

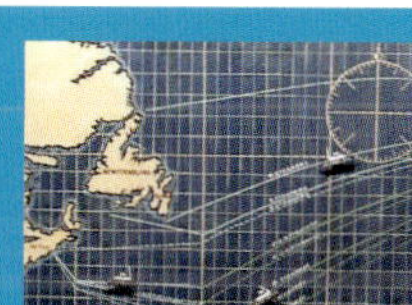

Map of the Bristol City Line Atlantic shipping routes **p38**

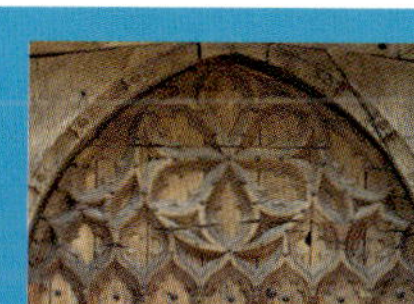

Spicer's Hall doorway **p35**

People Power

The activities of Bristol's people, both past and present, have defined the character for which it is known, as well as realising its successes and failures. Some have brought fame, fortune or notoriety to the city, while others have quietly achieved success, been inventive, creative or entrepreneurial. Nevertheless, they have collectively been responsible for making it the place that it is today.

Bristolians have seized many opportunities to make economic gain from trade, have created and challenged ethical and moral issues and have adapted to changing social and political contexts. The city's people continue to make it a place valued for its independent spirit, its wealth of culture and world-renowned festivals, its engineering and industrial heritage and particularly, in more recent years, its creative and media sectors.

The harbourside outside M Shed doubled as an Irish port for the 2019 film 'Stan & Ollie'. Bristol is a major centre of TV and film production. It is home to BBC Bristol and the world-renowned BBC Natural History Unit, as well as Academy Award-winning Aardman Animations and The Bottle Yard Studios.

Did you know?

Bristol was permanently designated UNESCO City of Film in 2017. This status celebrates Bristol's achievements as a leading city in the field of film and moving image. Bristol is a member of UNESCO's Creative Cities Network. It was awarded this accolade for its lasting contribution to film culture, production, heritage, education, research and technology.

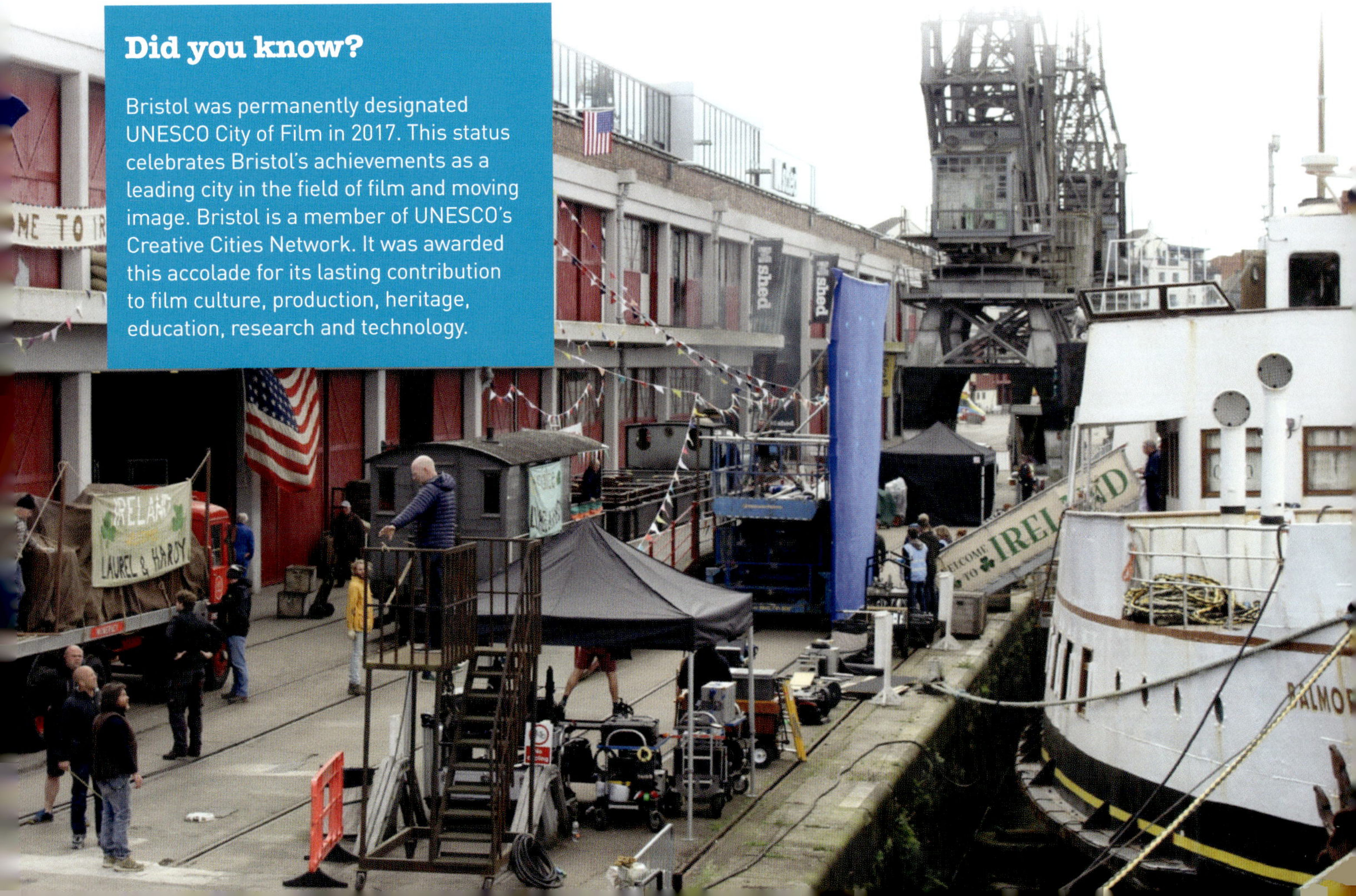

Trade

Bristol has been an important focus for trading activity for over a thousand years. By about 1250, it was the second most important port in the country after London, trading locally, nationally and internationally. Its people seized opportunities to trade in response to the forces of supply and demand, and this resulted in profits, losses and sometimes exploitation.

Bristol was built on the proceeds of international trade: until 1700, most of the trade was with Europe, but from 1700 to around 1840, it was geared towards the Americas and the West Indies via slavery and sugar. After 1840, Bristol's trade expanded worldwide.

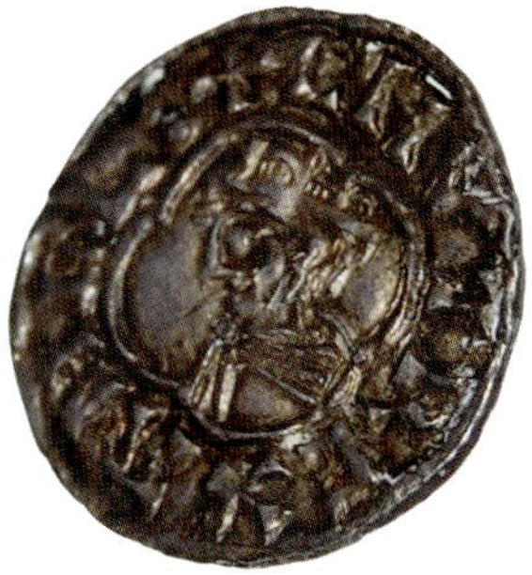

Silver penny of King Cnut. The importance of Bristol to early trade networks is demonstrated by the fact that it had a mint: this coin was produced in Bristol during the reign of King Cnut, 1017-1023. It was made by a moneyer called Aelfwine.

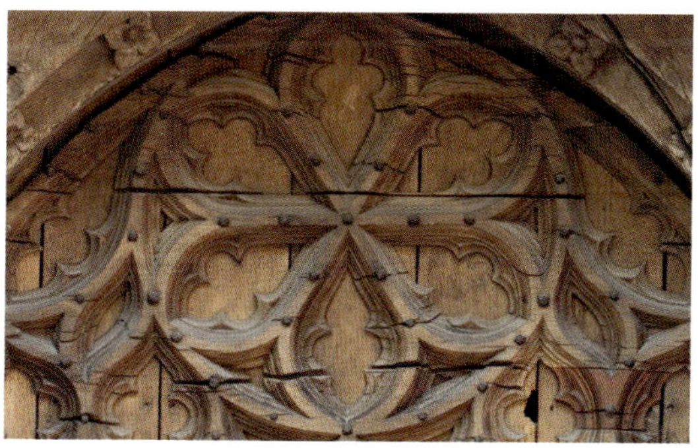

Tracery design on Spicer's door.

Did you know?

In the medieval period, merchants known as 'strangers' i.e. not 'freemen' of Bristol, were subject to many rules and regulations. They could only sell wholesale to Bristol merchants and their goods had to be stored and taxed centrally; after 1459, these goods were stored and sold in Spicer's Hall.

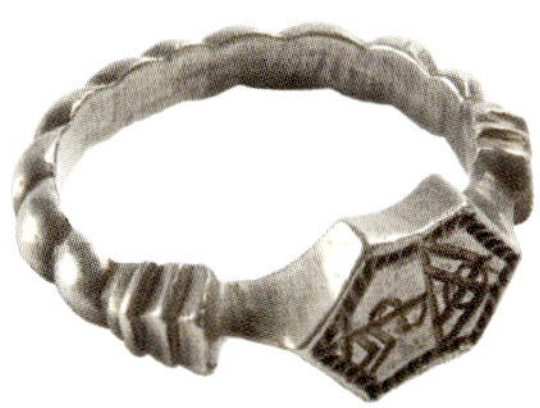

Silver ring with merchant's seal, about 1400, found near Alveston in South Gloucestershire. A merchant with the initials WS or SW wore this large silver ring on his gloved hand and used it seal documents or even parcels of goods. We don't know who he was or what he dealt in, but this valuable ring tells us that he was a successful.

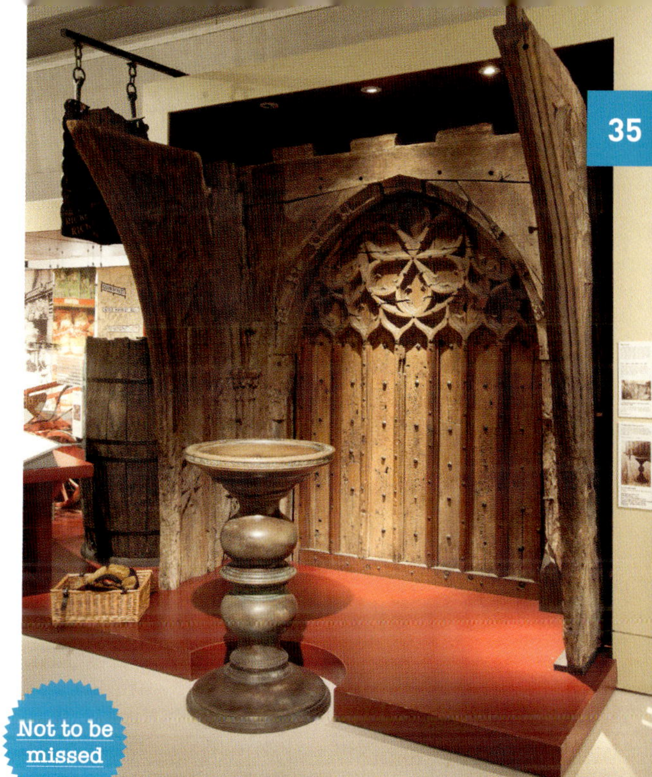

Not to be missed

© Quintin Lake Photography

Door to Spicer's Hall, about 1301-1350

This oak doorway was the entrance to Spicer's Hall, a medieval merchant's town house on Welsh Back, by Bristol Bridge. Richard Spicer was MP for Bristol in 1355 and three times Mayor. He bequeathed his home to the Mayor and Corporation of Bristol in 1377 and from 1459 it was used to store goods imported into the city by non-Bristolians, prior to sale.

The door is almost entirely oak except for some repairs. The earliest remaining feature is probably the tracery design, the upper section being carved from a single piece of timber. Most of the vertical bars below are replacements and many of the additions represent repairs in situ, including the latch, the keyhole and one of the hinges. The door may have been a later addition to the hall as the side bracket mouldings appear to be a style common to the late 1200s, while the tracery pattern on the door is similar to that used for church windows of the mid-1300s.

Bristol and the Transatlantic Slave Trade

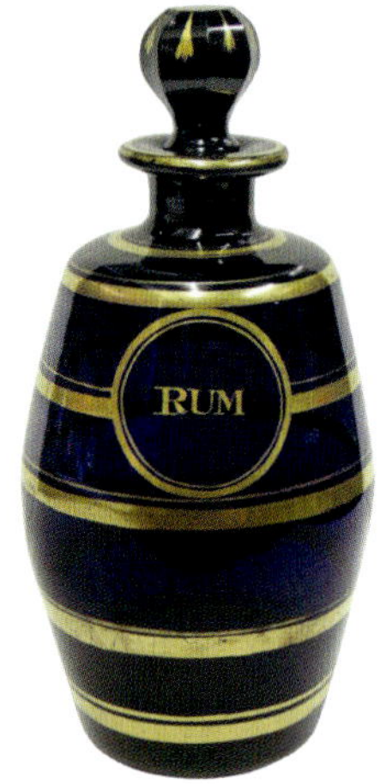

Rum decanter about 1785-1825. Imported commodities produced by enslaved people created jobs in old and new industries. Rum was a by-product of sugar refining, made in the Caribbean and in Britain. Local potteries and glassworks supplied the fine houses of the city with elegant containers such as ceramic sugar bowls and glass rum decanters.

For many years, the British trade in enslaved Africans to colonies in America and the Caribbean was run by London-based monopoly companies. Bristol's merchants campaigned to open up the trade, and when that happened in 1698, they became major players in the transatlantic slave trade, establishing trading systems and connections that others copied.

In the context of Bristol's long history as a trading port, the transatlantic slave trade lasted a relatively short time – but it was of great economic importance to the city. By the 1890s, the trade to Africa, America and the Caribbean was still estimated to account for 80% of the city's overseas trade.

Bristol ships carried over 500,000 African men, women and children into slavery in North and South America and the Caribbean. The transatlantic slave trade employed huge numbers in the city, in running the businesses, in outfitting the voyages, in crewing the ships and in processing the raw commodities brought home. It was a business in which human beings were treated as just another commodity to buy and sell.

Gallery tip: *Bristol and the Transatlantic Slave Trade is explored using multiple perspectives to highlight the complex web of involvement, relationships and thinking. A giant map explains details of the triangular route or 'great circuit'.*

Flintlock trade pistol, 1700s or early 1800s. Cotton cloth from India was the main item carried to Africa on a slaving ship, but a large part of the trade cargo consisted of guns and ammunition. Guns for the 'Africa trade' were often of poor quality.

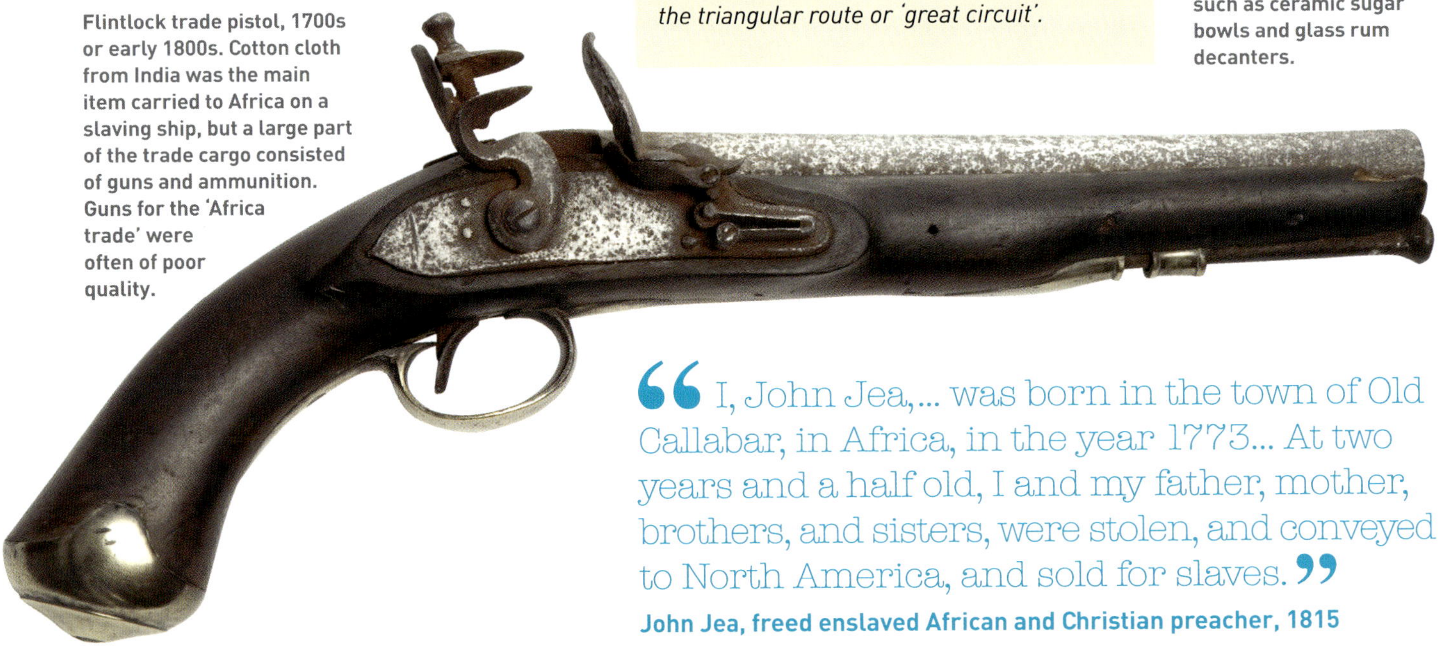

> "I, John Jea,... was born in the town of Old Callabar, in Africa, in the year 1773... At two years and a half old, I and my father, mother, brothers, and sisters, were stolen, and conveyed to North America, and sold for slaves."

John Jea, freed enslaved African and Christian preacher, 1815

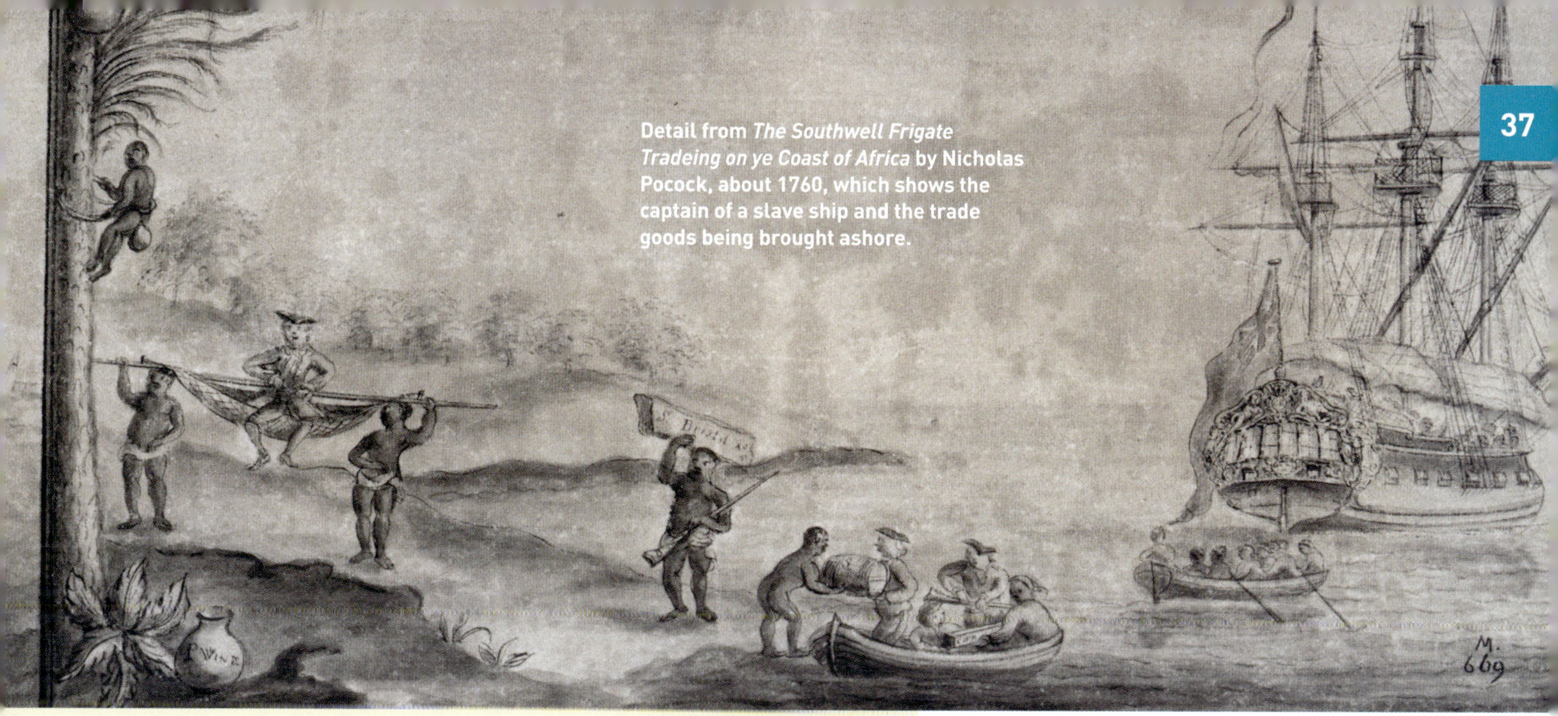

Detail from *The Southwell Frigate Tradeing on ye Coast of Africa* by Nicholas Pocock, about 1760, which shows the captain of a slave ship and the trade goods being brought ashore.

One small object... one large and terrible story

Merchants in Bristol bought glass beads from Venice and Bohemia (now part of the Czech Republic) and then traded them to Africa, where they formed part of the mix of trade goods used to buy enslaved men, women and children. In Africa, the glass beads were used to make jewellery and decorate clothing and insignia. In some areas, glass beads became an important part of the regalia of the kings and chiefs. African merchants particularly valued layered chevron beads and those with seven layers were the most valued. This six-layered chevron bead was made in Venice in the 1700s and was found in the mud of Bristol's Floating Harbour. This small glass bead links to the stories of all those involved in the transatlantic slave trade, from merchants and sailors to enslaved Africans and plantation owners to the people who took sugar in their tea – to the 2,018 known slaving voyages out of Bristol, and the 500,000+ enslaved Africans carried in those ships.

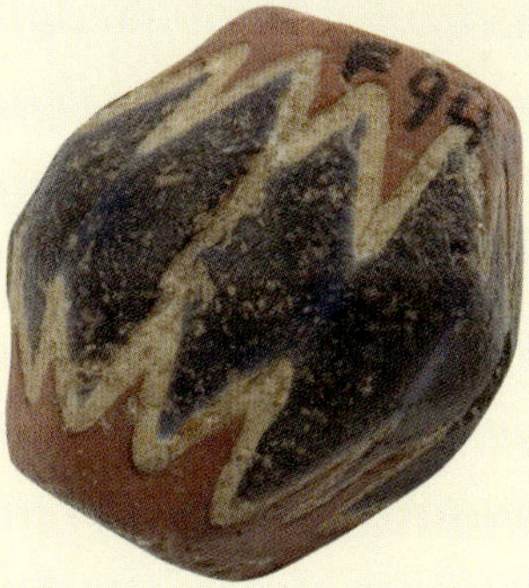

It's possible that this bead never made it to Africa or perhaps it did but was unused and returned to Bristol via the Caribbean. It must have been lost during the loading or unloading of a slave ship, before the Floating Harbour opened in 1809. It was found when the dock was drained or dredged many years later, long after an Act of Parliament ended the slave trade in 1807.

Iron box with the Abolition symbol, late 1700s

Supporters of the campaign to abolish the slave trade encouraged the use of their symbol to publicise the cause. It showed the enslaved African as a passive figure, asking for help from his white brothers and sisters. In fact, many enslaved Africans actively resisted slavery. Through open rebellion and quiet sabotage, they helped to make slavery uneconomic as a system of production, and turn public opinion against the slave trade.

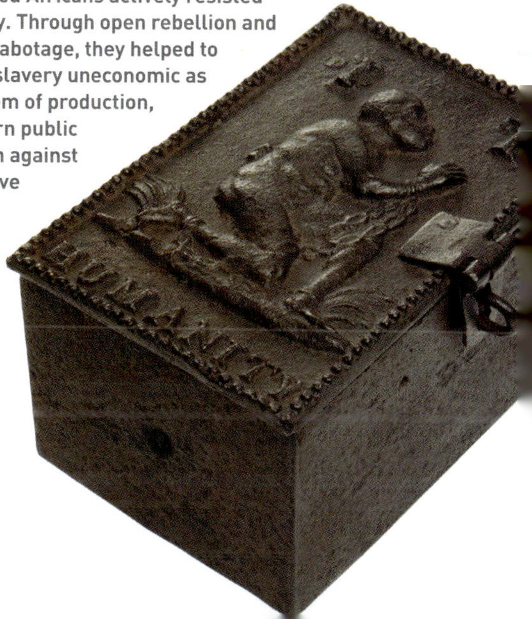

Trading by river...

Bristol's position relative to inland rivers made it a regional trade centre from about the year 1200 onwards, and merchants as well as merchandise came to the city. The River Severn provided a route inland to the Midlands and the north and Bristol became a distribution centre. Imported goods were taken up the river to sell and commodities such as woollen cloth and agricultural produce were brought back in return.

Did you know?

Abraham Darby, pioneer of the Industrial Revolution, established the Baptist Mills Brass Works in 1702. He experimented with casting brass and iron and he patented the process of using sand moulds. He then sold the brass works to Nehemiah Champion in the 1720s and moved back to the Midlands to concentrate on the Coalbrookdale ironworks.

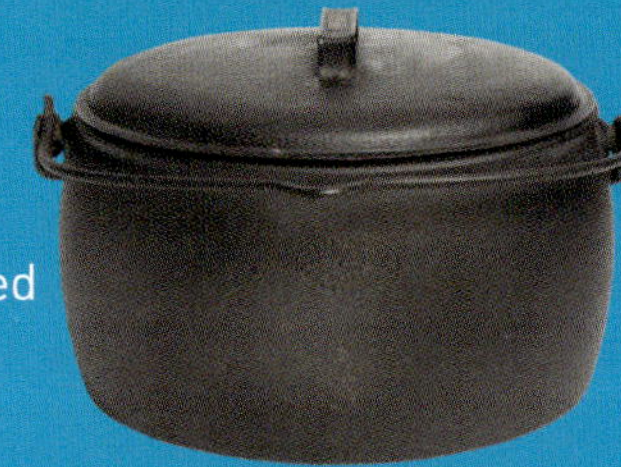

Cast iron pots were one of the exports from the industrial towns of the midlands via the River Severn, and Bristol and had a close link with Bristol through Abraham Darby.

...and by sea

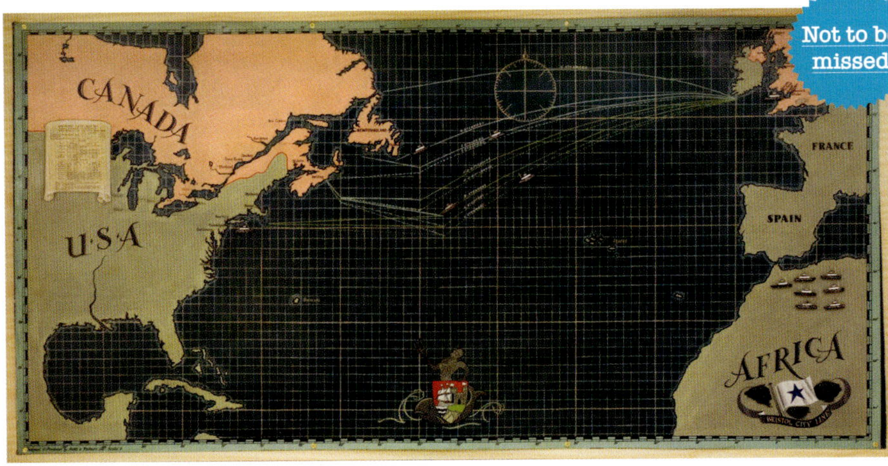

Not to be missed

Given by the National Maritime Museum (originally purchased with support from the National Heritage Memorial Fund)

Map of the Bristol City Line Atlantic shipping routes

The Bristol City Line of Steamships Ltd was a successful cargo fleet running ships from Bristol to New York, and later to most of the ports on the eastern seaboard of the USA and Canada. Staff used a tinplate map (left) to track the position of its vessels, which carried a distinctive blue-star flag and funnel marking.

Charles Hill took over the Hilhouse shipping and ship-building company in 1845. His company started The Bristol City Line of Steamships Ltd in 1879, firstly running steamships from Bristol to New York, in competition with Mark Whitwill's Great Western Steamship Line (although the City Line carried cargo rather than passengers). A service to Canada (Bristol - Quebec - Montreal) began in 1933, which was then extended to the Great Lakes in 1958. The company traded for almost 100 years until it was bought out by Bibby Line in 1972.

Bristol City Line's "Bristol City" arriving in New York with exports for the USA, accompanied by tugs. The Bristol City Line named all its ships after cities in Britain and the USA.

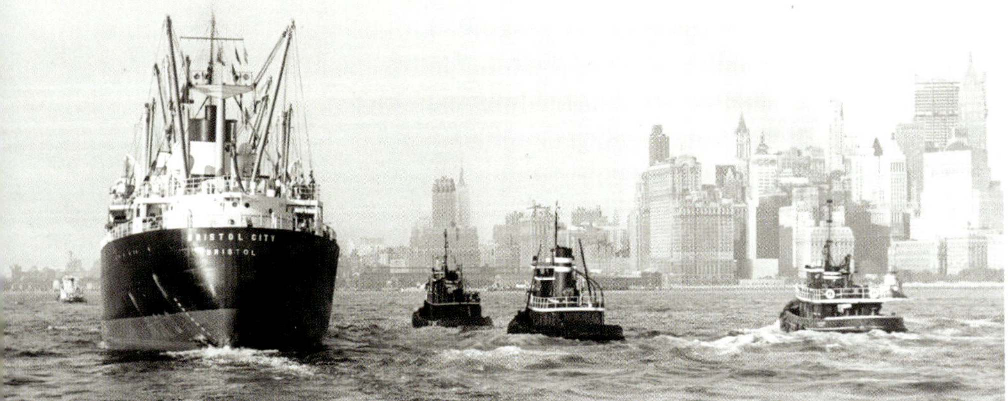

Challenging

Bristol people from all walks of life have been prepared to challenge the authorities, practices, philosophies and decision makers to effect social change or to right injustices.

Reform riots in Bristol

In October 1831, Bristol was the scene of some of the worst rioting ever witnessed in Britain, which was provoked by Parliament's opposition to electoral reform. Rioting also took place elsewhere, for example, in Nottingham. In Bristol, fires raged for three days, property was damaged and hundreds of people were injured or died. Troops were deployed to bring the situation under control. A new reform bill was finally passed in 1832.

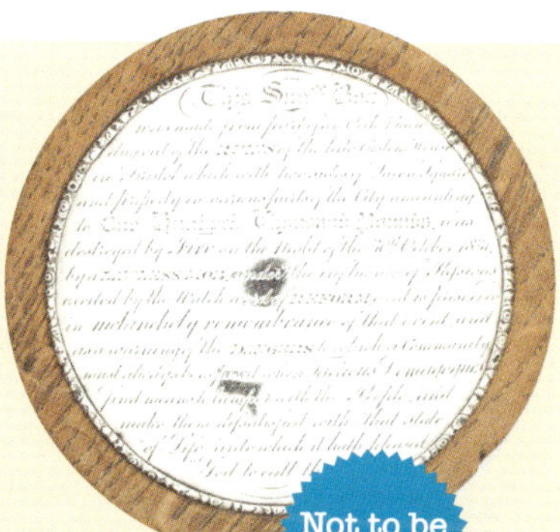

It's possible that more than one snuff box like this, with identically inscribed plaques, were produced.

Not to be missed

Snuff box – souvenirs of the 1831 Reform Riots

Local people collected a wide variety of souvenirs relevant to the riots. The silver plaque on this snuff box records that it is made from part of an oak beam dug out of the ruins from the destroyed Custom House, which was one of a number of buildings to be looted and burned in Queen Square. However, while this souvenir might seem relatively innocuous, others were less so, and include a human upper arm bone that was inscribed and carved at one end.

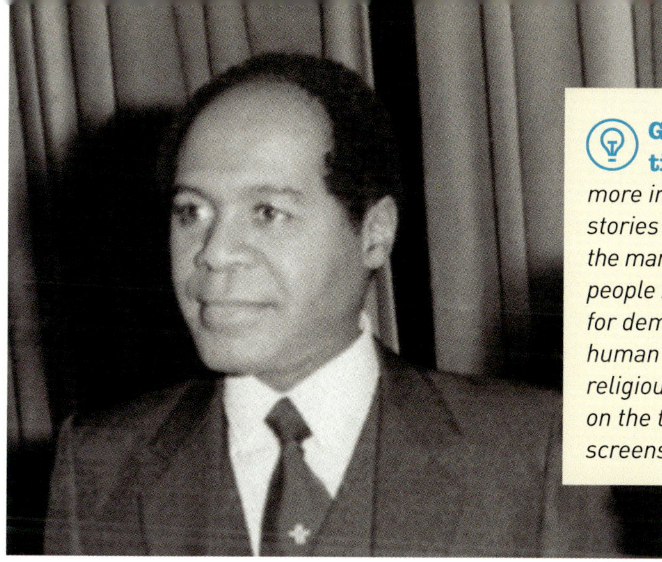

Gallery tip: *explore more images and stories that detail the many ways that people have fought for democracy, human rights or religious reform on the touch screens.*

Paul Stephenson has received many awards and honours including an OBE in 2009 for services to equal opportunities and community relations in Bristol. © Paul Stephenson

Bristol Bus Boycott

There were no laws against racial discrimination in Britain until 1965. In 1963, local Black campaigners in Bristol exposed the Bristol Omnibus Company's refusal to employ Black workers as bus drivers or conductors. Paul Stephenson, who was then a youth worker in Bristol and spokesperson for the campaigners, organised a bus boycott inspired by the American civil rights movement. The dispute captured international press attention and, after four months, the Bristol Omnibus Company eventually agreed to hire Black workers.

Sugar boycott

A national movement to boycott sugar and other plantation goods was started in 1791 to support the slave trade abolition campaign. Mary Anne Galton (later Mrs Schimmelpenninck) moved to Bristol in 1806 and was one of many women who abstained from sugar as a protest in her youth. Enslaved Africans did the hard work of cultivating and processing sugar cane on plantations. Sugar abstinence was an activity where women took the lead; they ran the household and could decide what products to buy.

The sugar boycott was a small part of a long campaign to which many people contributed. Eventually Parliament passed an Act to abolish the slave-trade in 1807 and another to emancipate the enslaved in 1834. Medallions were struck to mark both events and to communicate the anti-slavery message.

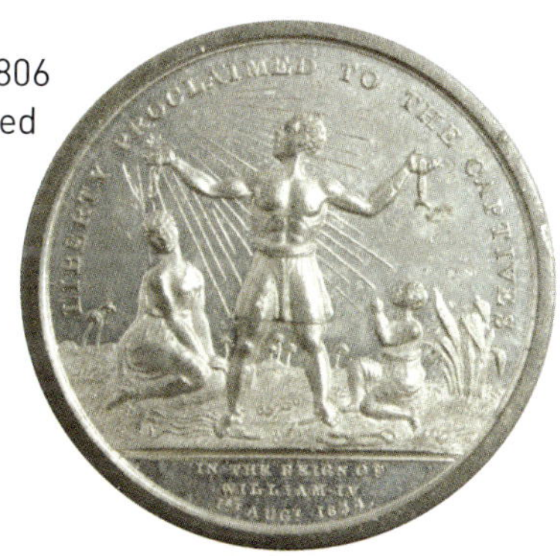

Creating

Bristol's people have been, and continue to be, responsible for many ideas, products and processes, from the artistic to the industrial to the scientific, and they continue to push the boundaries in terms of their creative ingenuity and resourcefulness.

Gallery tip: *you can find out more about the Great Western Railway and the Clifton Suspension Bridge in the Bristol Places gallery.*

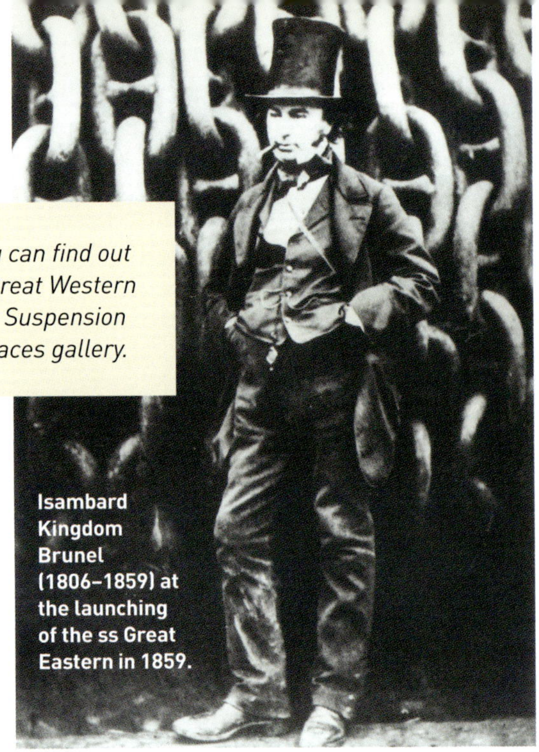

Isambard Kingdom Brunel (1806–1859) at the launching of the ss Great Eastern in 1859.

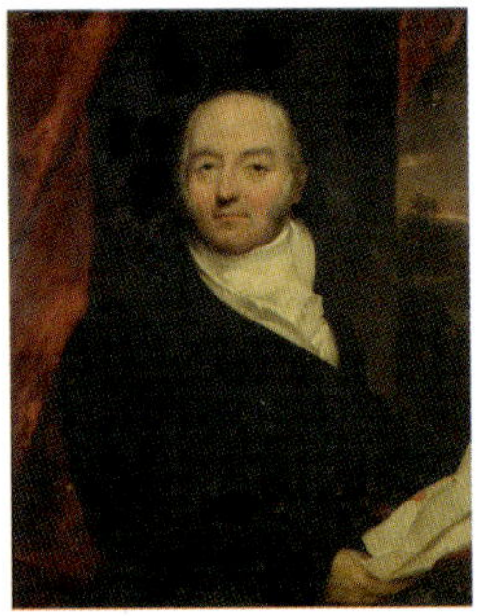

Portrait of Isaac Jacobs (1757/8–1835) by Isaac Pocock.

Bristol Blue Glass

Not to be missed

Blue glass was made in Bristol between the late 1700s and the 1820s and then began to be manufactured again in the 1980s.

Lazarus Jacobs came to Bristol in the 1760s from Frankurt-am-Main. By 1774 he had set up a glass engraving business with his son Isaac in Temple Street, which is where they began to manufacture 'Bristol Blue'. The rich blue colour was created by the addition of cobalt oxide to the glass mix and the vessels that resulted were also enhanced with hand-painted gilded designs, making them a luxury product. The demand for blue glass grew rapidly and by 1787 Lazarus had moved to larger premises in Avon Street. When he died in 1796, at the age of 87, the business passed to his son Isaac. Isaac elevated the production of Bristol Blue to a higher level. However by the mid-1820s, the business had closed, foreshadowing the decline of the city's glass industry in the following decades.

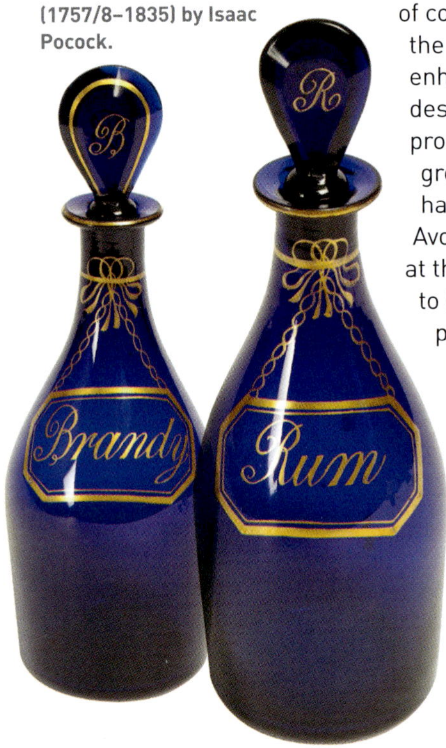

Blue glass decanters, about 1810, made in Bristol by the Jacobs family. Isaac Jacobs was unusual at the time in signing his wares.

Isambard Kingdom Brunel (1806-1859)

Although not Bristol born and bred, much of Brunel's work is synonymous with the city, from the design of the iconic Clifton Suspension Bridge to the engineering of the Great Western Railway, among many others. Brunel also designed the world's first large iron propeller-driven steam ship, the Great Britain, which now rests in the dock where she was built, just along the quayside from M Shed.

Did you know?

Brunel's paddle steamer Great Western was launched from the quayside where M Shed now stands. Designed by Brunel and built by William Patterson, she was the largest wooden ship in the world at that time. She carried people and cargo across the Atlantic until 1852.

Not to be missed

Bristol Pegasus engine

Bristol and its engineers have been at the forefront of aero engine development since the 1920s. The Bristol Pegasus engine is a nine-cylinder, single-row, air-cooled radial aero engine that was designed by Roy Fedden and Leonard 'Bunny' Butler, of the Bristol Aeroplane Company, in 1932. It was used in both civil and military aircraft in the 1930s and 1940s, including combat aircraft in World War II. It was also used in several record-breaking aircraft, which broke altitude and distance records in the 1930s, and powered the first aircraft to fly over Mt Everest.

Gallery tip: *don't forget to press the button to see the moving parts of the engine in action.*

Working scale model of a 'jump jet' engine lent by the Rolls-Royce Heritage Trust: this Bristol-Siddeley engine, which powered the vertical take-off Harrier jet, was also given the name Pegasus but is a very different type of engine.

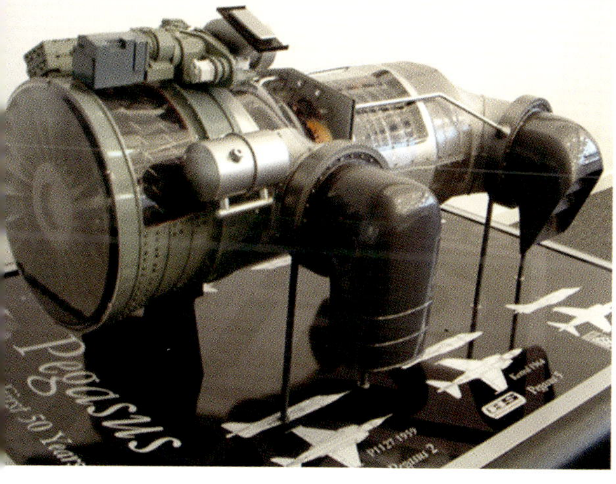

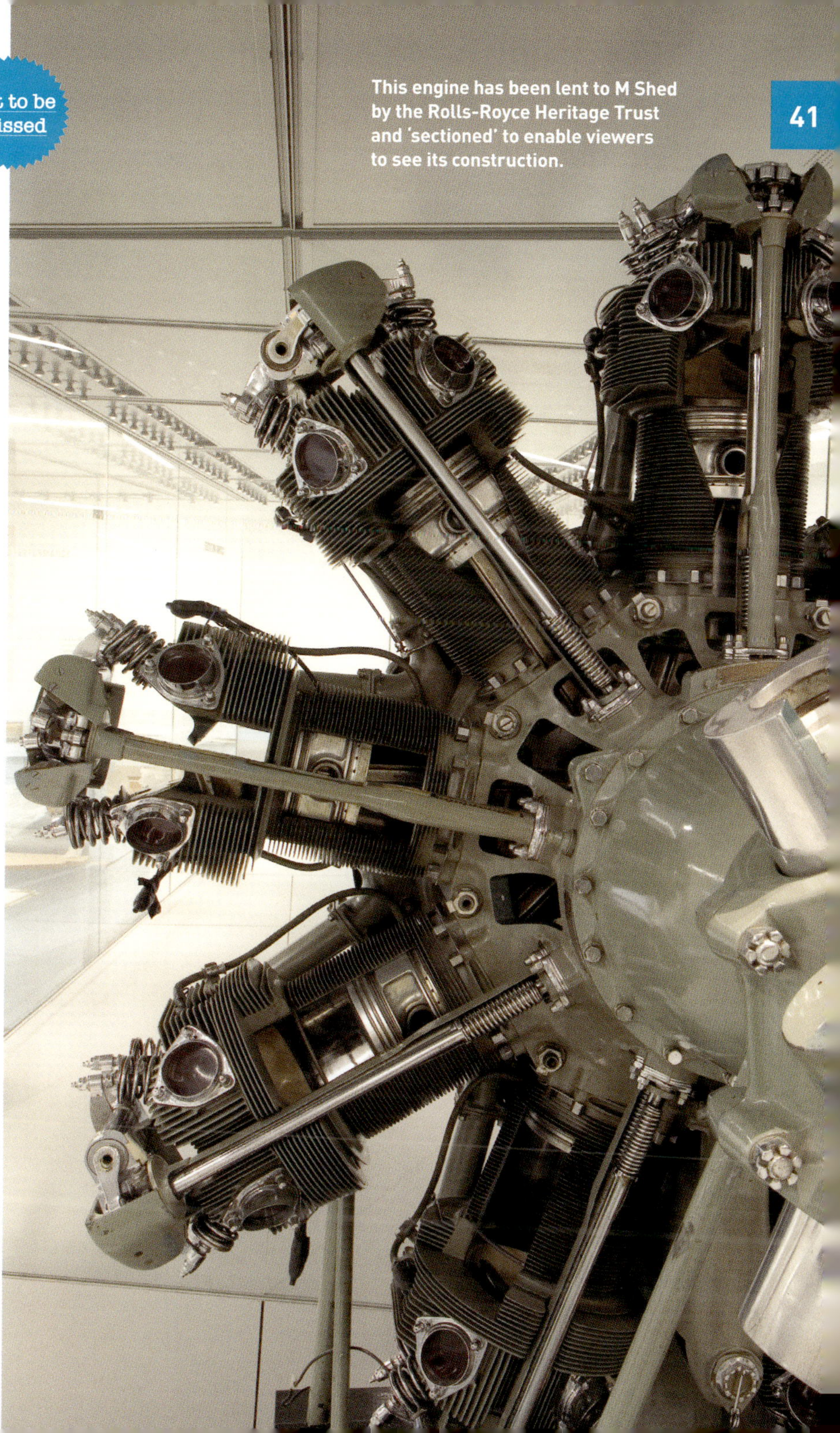

This engine has been lent to M Shed by the Rolls-Royce Heritage Trust and 'sectioned' to enable viewers to see its construction.

Celebrating

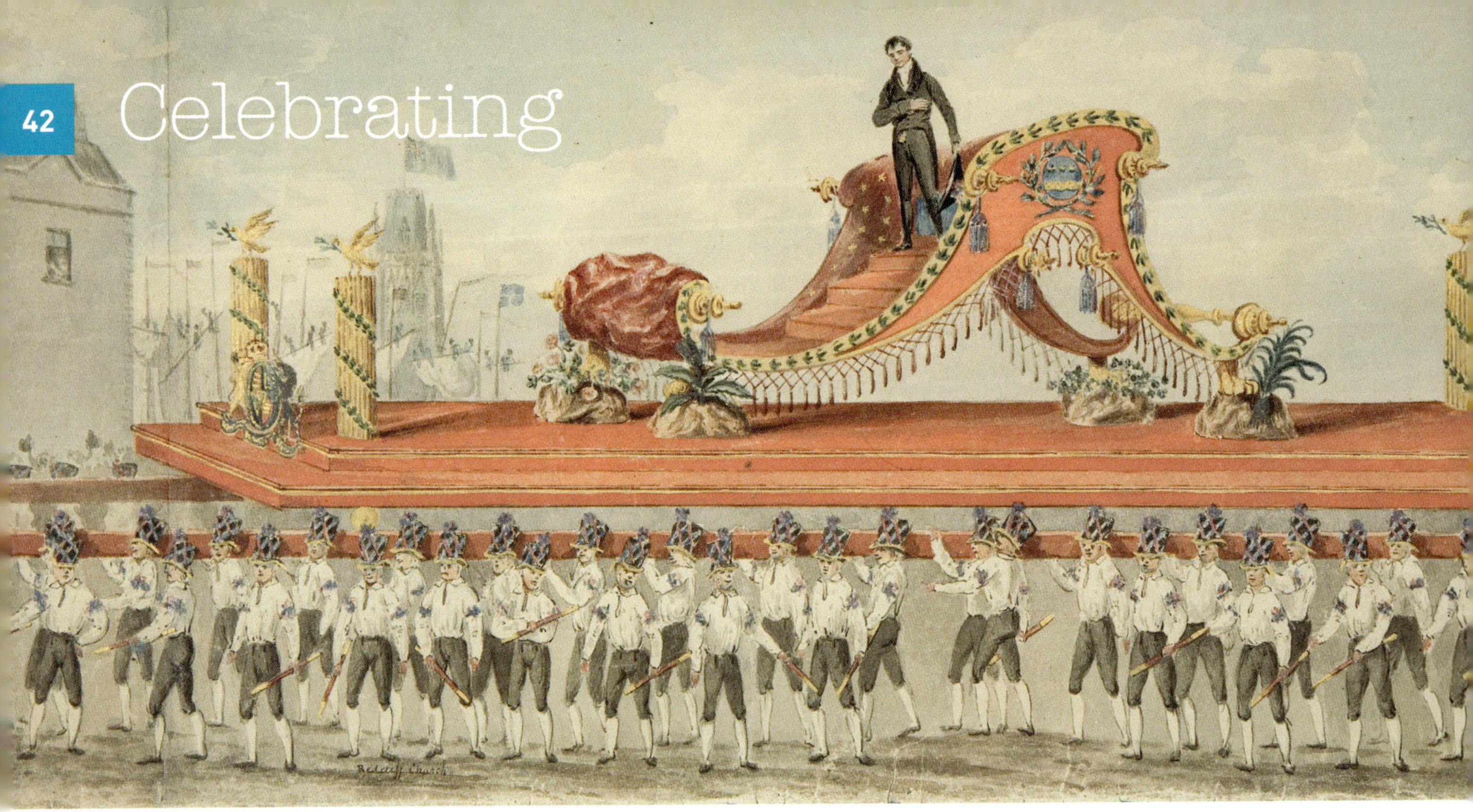

From fiestas to parades, the people of Bristol have always known how to enjoy themselves and show other people how to have a good time too. They gather together to reinforce their community identity, express their faith and to create festivals and events that are acclaimed at home as well as abroad.

The Chairing of Henry Bright, 10 March 1820 by Henry Smith (about 1775-1840)

Not to be missed

The General Election of 1820 was strongly contested in Bristol and while the process itself was widely regarded as corrupt, the 'chairing' ceremony that signified the acceptance of the newly-elected representative was lavish, colourful and fun. Henry Bright, a Whig, was the winner and was 'chaired', or paraded, through the streets.

Gallery tip: *immerse yourself in the sights and sounds of Bristol's world famous festivals and events by taking a seat to watch them unfold on the gallery's big screen.*

The whole procession, which started near St Stephen's Church, is reported to have taken 3.5 hours to make its way back to the beginning. The line of people carrying various banners and insignia of commerce and shipping was enhanced by the noise of bands playing, cannon fire and church bells. At that time, only those men with the freedom of the city could vote but the volume of cheering crowds suggested everyone enjoyed the parade, even if they couldn't vote for a candidate.

Henry Bright was MP for Bristol 1820-1830 and his family had extensive financial interests in slave-trading and West Indian plantations. In 1823 he was part of a committee formed to press for 'ameliorationist' measures for the Crown colonies and to resist moves towards emancipation of slaves.

Chinese New Year

Watercolour of a Lion Dance, 1850-1900. Two children are dancing in a lion costume, while another is dressed up in a white mask as 'Big Head Buddha' (da tou fo) to attract its attention. Acquired through the Art Fund from the J O Thompson bequest.

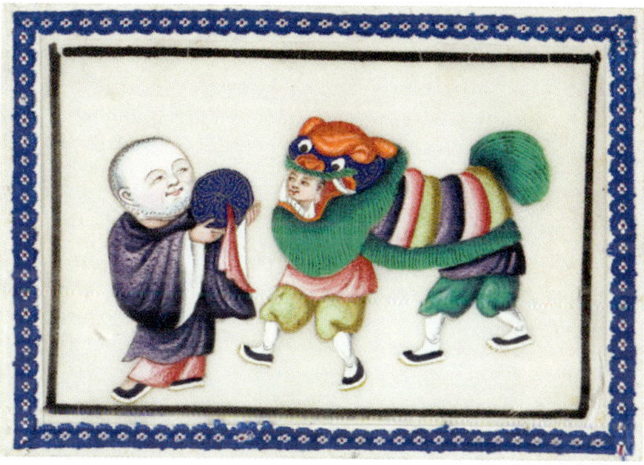

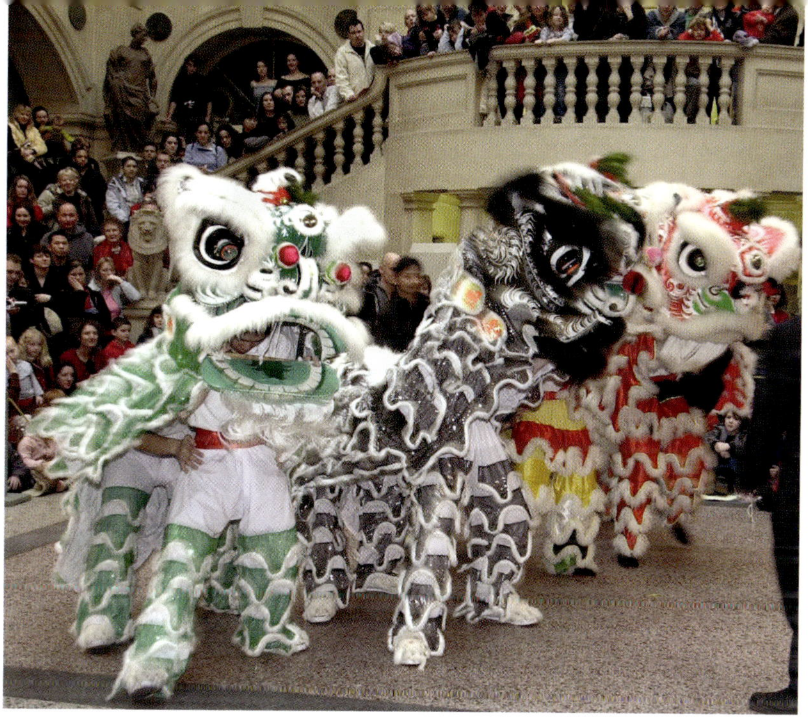

A traditional lion dance being performed at Bristol Museum & Art Gallery.

The lunar New Year is celebrated by Chinese people worldwide, and the largest celebration in South West England takes place at Bristol Museum & Art Gallery. Museum staff, local people and students have worked together to share their enthusiasm about Chinese culture for over 20 years. This two-day event, which takes place in February, consists of a programme of spectacular traditional and contemporary performances, stalls, workshops and activities and attracts up to 9,000 visitors per year. Performances by the University of Bristol Chinese Lion Dance Troupe are a highlight of the celebrations.

Flying high – Bristol's International Balloon Fiesta

Bristol's first demonstration balloon flight took off from a field behind Stoke's Croft in 1810, but Europe's largest meeting of hot air balloons now takes place every year at Ashton Court Estate. It started life with just 29 hot air balloons in the late 1970s but now attracts over 130 balloons and pilots from all over the world. A sky full of hot air balloons flying over Bristol's iconic Clifton Suspension Bridge is a sight to behold.

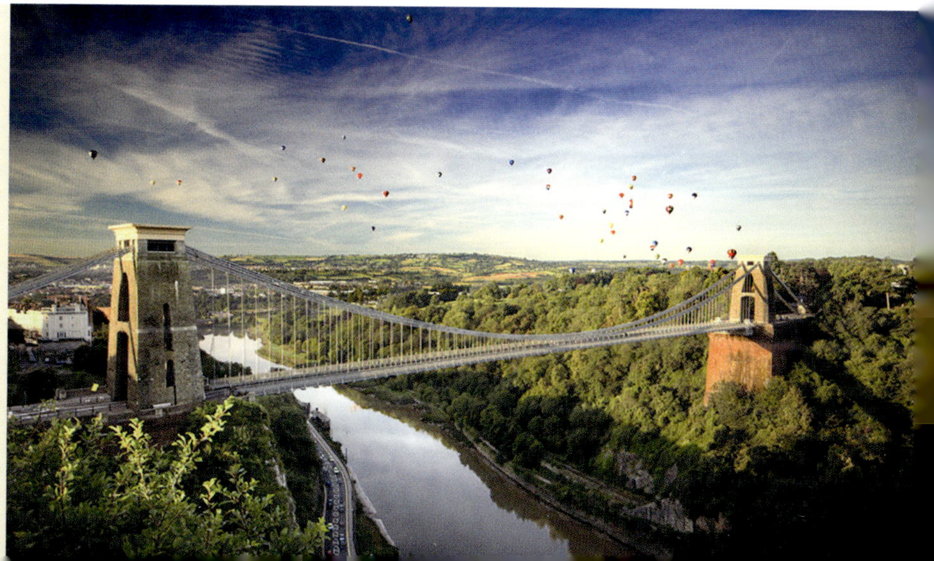

Mass balloon ascents are a feature of Bristol's Balloon Fiesta...weather permitting! © Gary Newman, Destination Bristol

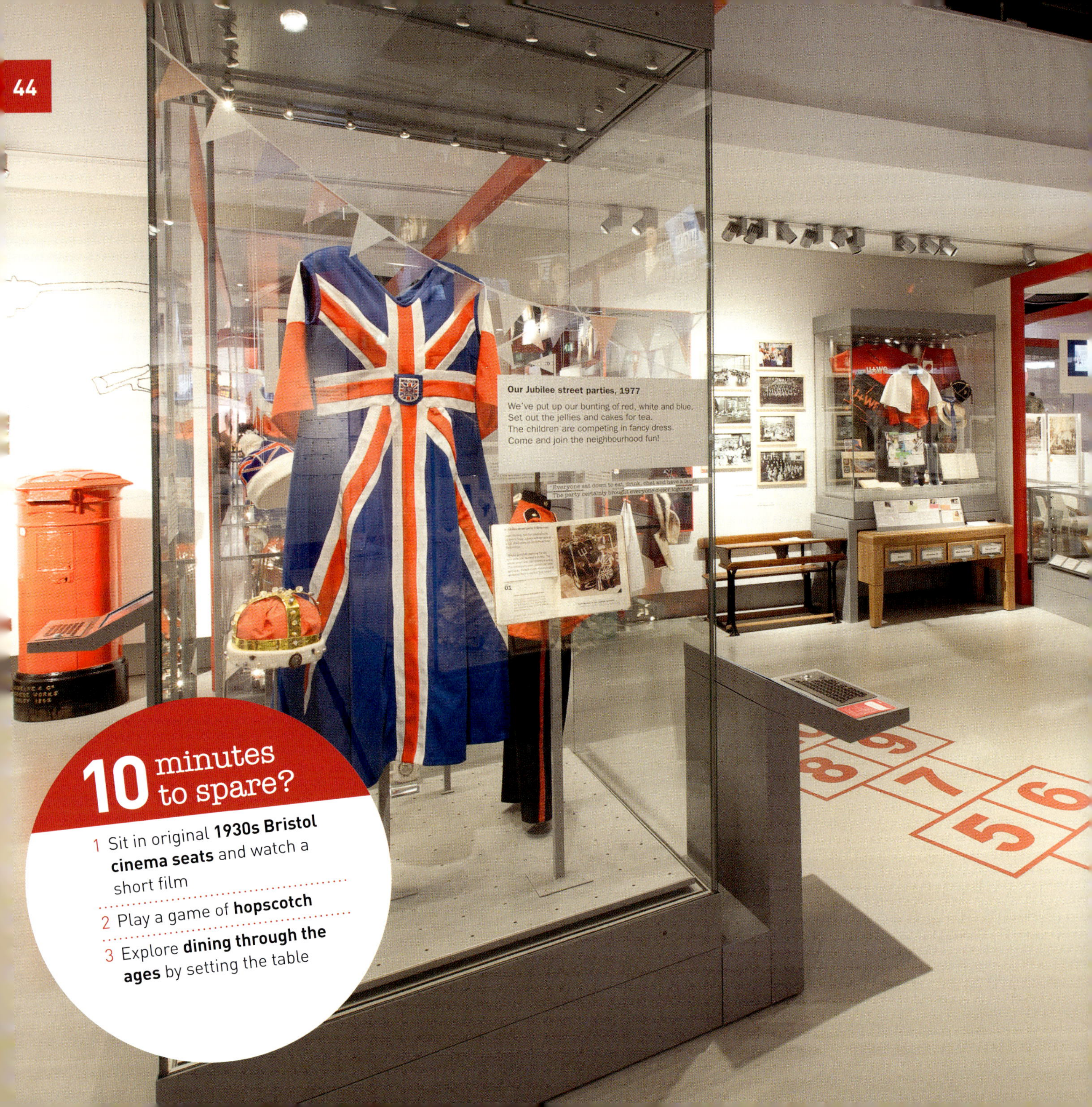

10 minutes to spare?

1 Sit in original **1930s Bristol cinema seats** and watch a short film

2 Play a game of **hopscotch**

3 Explore **dining through the ages** by setting the table

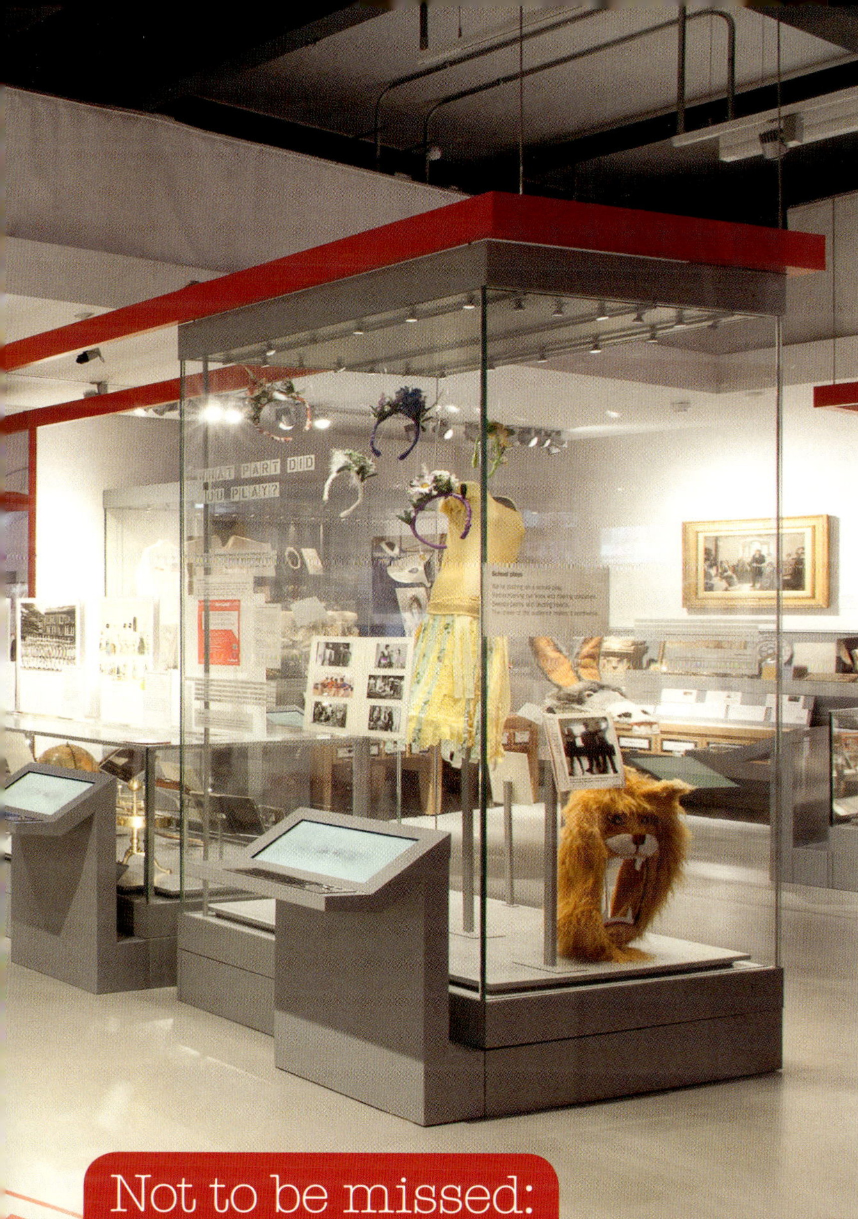

© Quintin Lake Photography

M Shed's galleries at a glance:

Bristol Life

This gallery explores the many ways in which people connect socially with each other in Bristol, whether with family and neighbours, at work, in school or out on the town in one of its venues. It explores themes relating to:

- **Joining and leaving**
- **In our houses**
- **Down our streets**
- **In our classrooms**
- **In our workplaces**
- **Out in the city**

Visitors can find out more about:

- Belonging, identity and diversity
- Experiences shared by family and friends
- Activities people enjoy together
- Workplace experiences and relationships
- Unforgettable special days and nights
- Personal stories about communities of faith

Not to be missed:

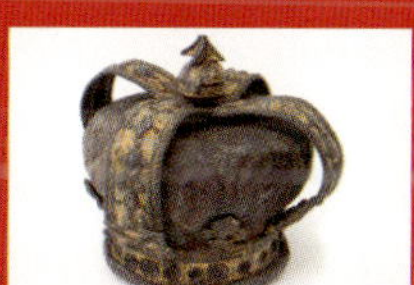

Billo's crown
p47

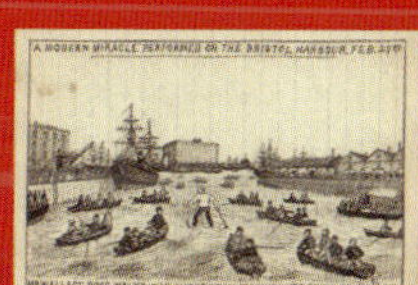

Diary of Harry Bow
p56

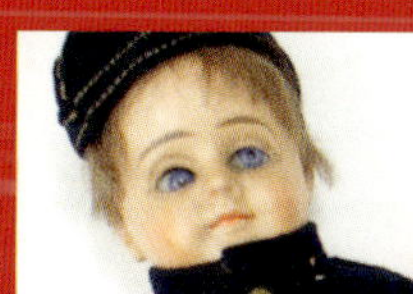

Victorian industrial school doll
p52

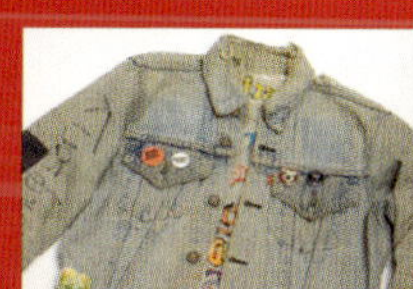

Denim jacket
p56

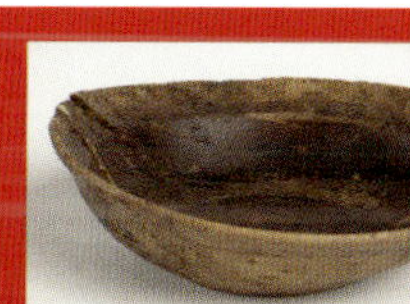

Wooden monastic bowls
p50

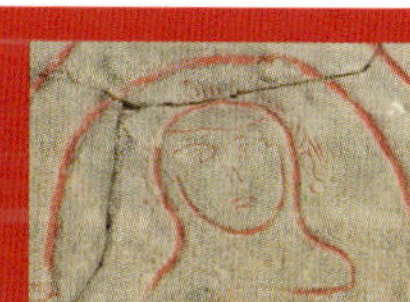

Roman tombstone
p46

That's Life

Bristol's population has become increasingly diverse. Its people originate from over 180 countries of birth, with 91 main languages and at least 45 religions. Nevertheless, what connects the people of Bristol are the ways that they socialise with other, at home, at work and at leisure, and their shared values, relationships and experiences.

Joining and leaving

Bristol has always had a diverse and shifting population with a long history of migration. All the people born here, or who have arrived from elsewhere, are part of its history. They contribute to the make-up of its communities and cultural identity. There are certainly those who consider themselves Bristol 'born and bred' but it's entirely possible they have ancestors or relatives that were drawn here in the past, to trade, to seek a new life, to study, marry, work or to seek refuge. Conversely, there are others who have chosen to leave to make their fortunes elsewhere or who, at times, were removed against their will.

Did you know?

Up until the 1960s the single largest immigrant group in Bristol was the Welsh. There is an area of quayside in Bristol that is still called 'Welsh Back' as this was a focus for Welsh trade and traders.

South Side of King Street with Llandoger Trow, **by Thomas Leeson Rowbotham, about 1825. This tavern, built in 1664, may have taken its name from LLandogo, a village upstream on the River Wye in South Wales.**

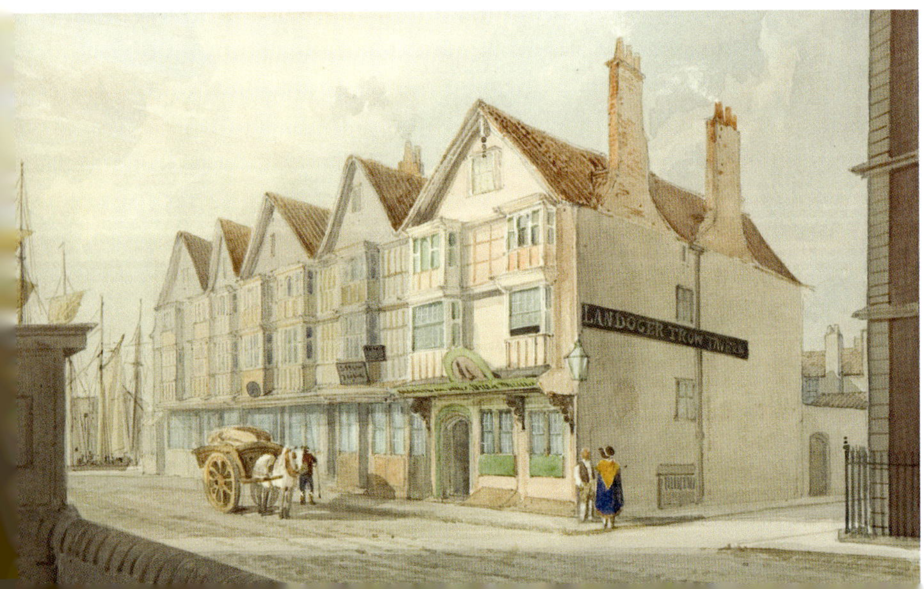

Did Gaius' family come from Gaul (France)? The dog and cockerel may be symbols of rebirth but the star is like those found on tombstones in Gaul and coincidentally the Latin word for a rooster is 'gallus'.

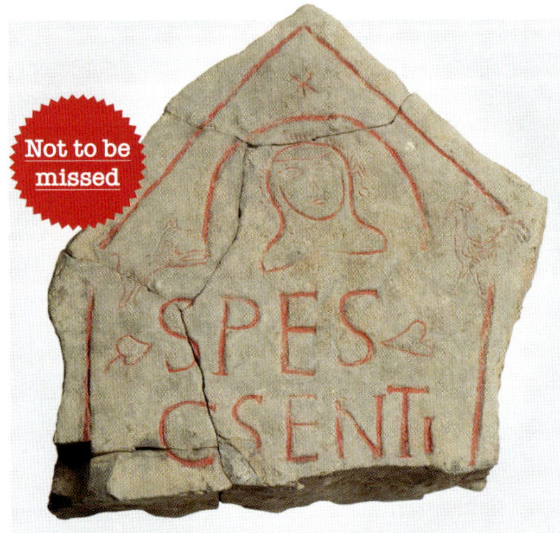

Roman tombstone found at Sea Mills

Labourers working on a plateau overlooking Sea Mills in 1873 uncovered the skeletal remains of a young woman beneath this inscribed and decorated Roman tombstone. Examination of the woman's remains showed that she was 20-25 years old when she died. The letters read 'SPES C SENTI', which means either the 'wife' or 'daughter', or 'the hope' of Gaius Sentius. We can only guess as to who Gaius was or where he came from. He could have been here as a trader or descended from a soldier from another part of the Roman Empire. Whoever he was, he is the earliest person in the Bristol area for whom we have a name, and he buried a loved-one here about 1,700 years ago.

Gallery tip: *ask staff at M Shed for details about how to visit Bristol's Kings Weston Roman Villa and find out more about it in the Bristol Places Gallery.*

Some who arrived...

Some people have chosen to come to Bristol, some have fled from persecution and some were brought here against their will. Here are a few examples of their stories.

Lilleith Morrison's suitcase

Lilleith Morrison came to England from Jamaica in 1955 when she was just seven-years-old. Her father had been posted to England as a soldier during World War II and later decided to return here with his family in 1954. Lilleith brought this suitcase with her when she travelled to England with her brothers and her nanny, who was a young woman called Castor. Unlike their parents, who came by ship, the children travelled by plane and landed at Heathrow. The suitcase is embossed with an image of Queen Elizabeth II and the date of her coronation. Lilleith recalled that "As long as I could remember I'd known about England. I'd even been encouraged to keep a scrapbook of newspaper cuttings of the Queen's Coronation."

Lilleith Morrison's suitcase. Lilleith came to Bristol in 1981, and in 1983 she pioneered the teaching of Black History in Further Education. Among her many other achievements, she co-wrote 'Memoirs of a Black Englishman' with Paul Stephenson, published in 2011.

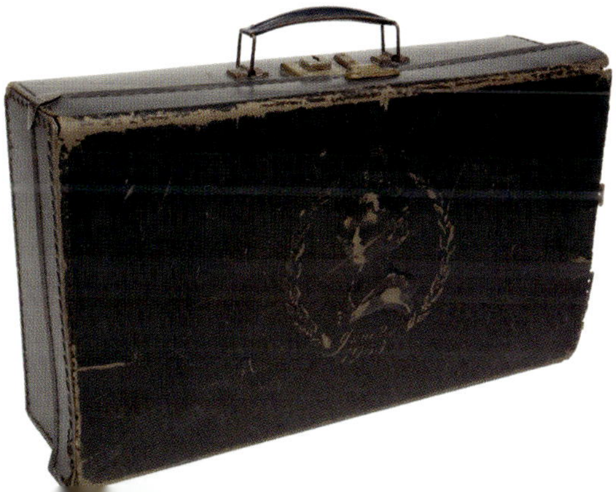

Billo's crown, 1733

Not to be missed

Francis Billo made this copper alloy replica of the English royal crown as a gift for his parish church of St Stephen's. It was originally gilded, painted red and encrusted with imitation jewels, but sadly these are now missing. Billo is believed to have been a 'Huguenot' (French Protestant) and was a skilled brass worker who became known for his chandeliers. Around 400-500 Huguenots came to Bristol in the late 1600s, fleeing persecution by the French authorities, who wanted to force them to convert to Catholicism. In 1720, Billo was accepted as a 'burgess' (a freeman of the City of Bristol) by making a 'cistern and a fountain of his own workmanship' instead of paying the usual £15 fee (about six months' wages).

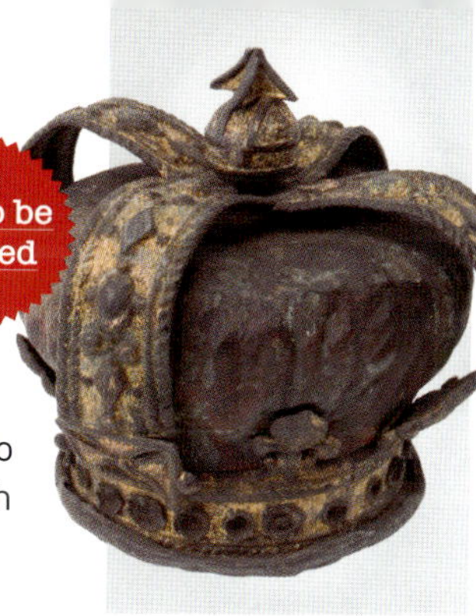

This crown may also have been used for trade processions, although a watercolour dated to 1734 clearly shows it on display at St. Stephen's Church.

Inuit in Bristol

Three Inuit abducted from Nunavut (Northern Canada) were brought back to Bristol in 1577 by Captain Martin Frobisher when he returned from an expedition to find the 'Northwest Passage'. The man, woman and her baby boy were known as 'Calichough', 'Ignorth' and 'Nutiok', although these were not their proper names. The Mayor of Bristol gave a reception where Calichough demonstrated his kayaking and hunting skills on the River Avon. Sadly, all three soon died of infectious diseases. Calichough and Ignorth are buried in St Stephen's churchyard in Bristol while Nutiok is buried at St Olave's Church in London. In 2018, a project to critically and culturally respond to Frobisher's voyages to Nunavut, and which aims to acknowledge the legacy of the lives of these three Inuit, was underway.

Sealskin parka, 1801-1900. This sealskin parka is similar to the one Calichough was wearing when he arrived in Bristol.

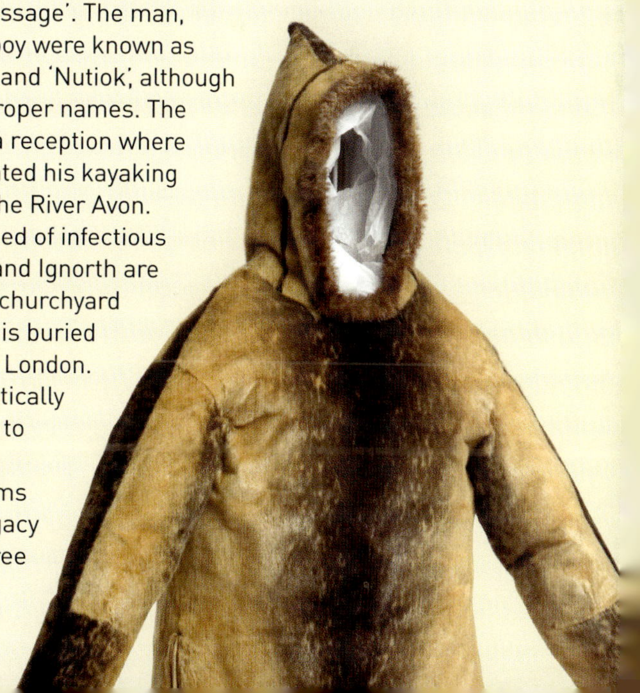

...and some who left

The grass is sometimes greener for people who have chosen to leave Bristol, but for others there was no choice.

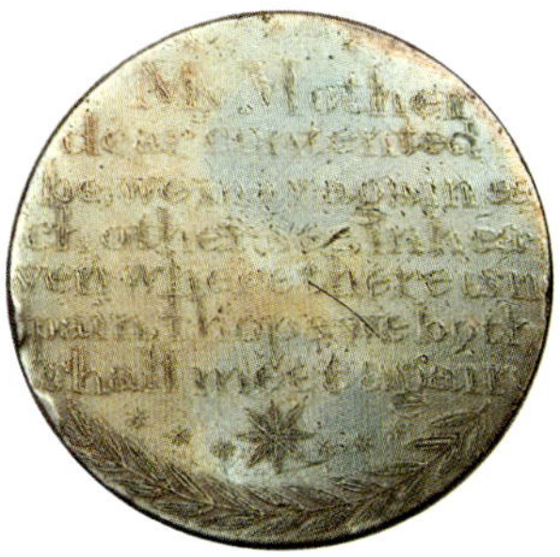

Jabez Hill's convict token, 1820. Like many other convicts awaiting transportation to Australia, Jabez gave an engraved metal token to his mother as keepsake.

Jabez Hill – transported to Australia

Jabez Hill was just 19-years-old when he was sentenced to death in 1820. He and another teenager broke into Bristol's Blind Asylum and stole £46, the equivalent value of a labourer's annual wage. Hill's sentence was commuted from death to transportation for life to Australia. His journey, along with 171 other convicts on board a ship called Elizabeth II, took almost 3.5 months. Hill had no real hope of seeing his family again. Transportation took the pressure off overcrowded British prisons and the convicts provided a cheap source of labour with which to build the new colony. Hill married and had children in Australia, and received a conditional discharge in 1850. His descendants still live there today.

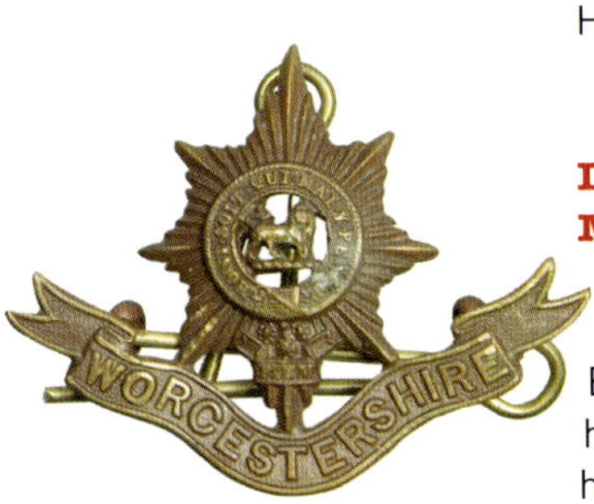

Stanley Booker's regimental cap badge. Stanley initially volunteered for the Gloucester Regiment's Citizens' Battalion, which was popularly known as 'Bristol's Own'. In transferred to the Worcestershire Regiment in 1915.
Bristol Archives 40715/Pers/SCB/7/2

Lieutenant Stanley Charles Booker MC (1893-1916)

Like many others who volunteered for active service during World War I, Stanley Booker hoped that he would return safely home to his family in Bristol. Unfortunately he was killed in action in France in October 1916, having been hit by a sniper's bullet as part of a rescue party sent out to search for wounded men. In the last letter he wrote to his mother before embarkation, he said "If God wills I shall come back to you safe and sound; if I do not, why there is nothing hard in dying for a great cause, after all it is the cause that matters and not the life of this individual or that." Stanley was just one of the 6,648 men enlisted in Bristol who were killed during World War I.

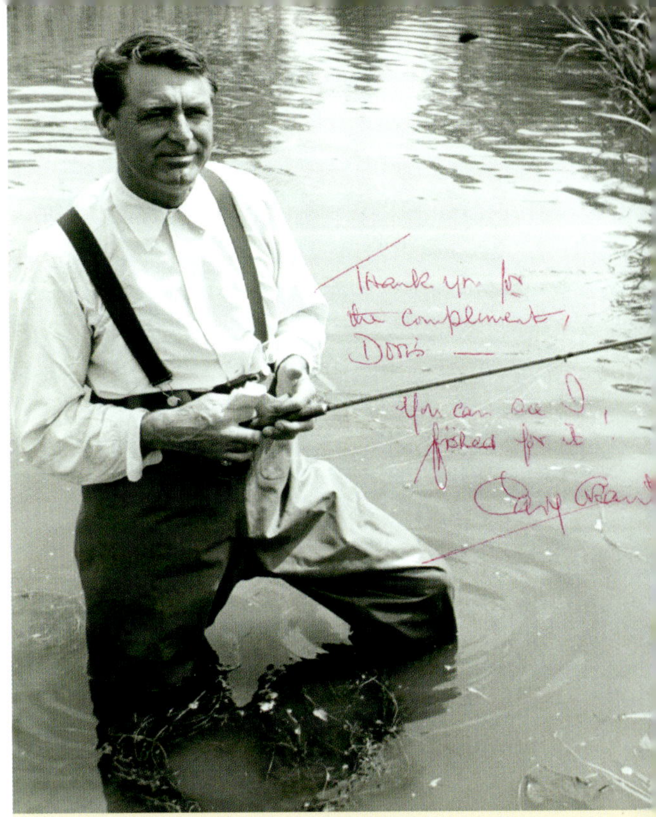

Signed photograph of Cary Grant sent to Doris, a fan from St Paul's, Bristol who had won the right to meet him.
Bristol Archives 41006/Ph/2/12(a)

Archibald Alec Leach – Cary Grant (1904-1986)

Many aspiring actors have needed to move to London or Hollywood to fulfil their ambitions. Archibald Alec Leach, better known as Cary Grant, was born in Horfield, Bristol, in 1904. He attended Bishop Road School and later received a scholarship to Fairfield Grammar School. A weekend job at the Hippodrome theatre provided an escape from family tensions and sowed the seeds for a career in acting. He joined the Bob Pender stage troupe in 1919, having engineered his expulsion from school, and toured the United States with them. When the rest of the troupe returned to Europe, Archie decided to stay in America and eventually found success in Hollywood.

At home

Homes are the hub of household and family activities; they provide a place for people who live together to eat, sleep, talk and be entertained, as well as somewhere to clean, cook and mend. No matter what the make-up of particular households, there are experiences that many Bristolians share with each other and across time.

Everyday experiences

People who live together today usually share domestic responsibilities and now use electrical appliances to make housework easier. In the past, it was largely the role of women to attend to cleaning, childcare and general housework. A modern household might also take advantage of convenience food or takeaways rather than cooking at home. Nevertheless there has always been a need for domestic utensils and tableware and many of these have been produced in Bristol. As for entertainment, before the arrival of radio, TV and the Internet, many people entertained themselves at home by playing games, telling stories, singing, and catching up on the daily news. In some households it is also important to parents that children continue to understand their family heritage.

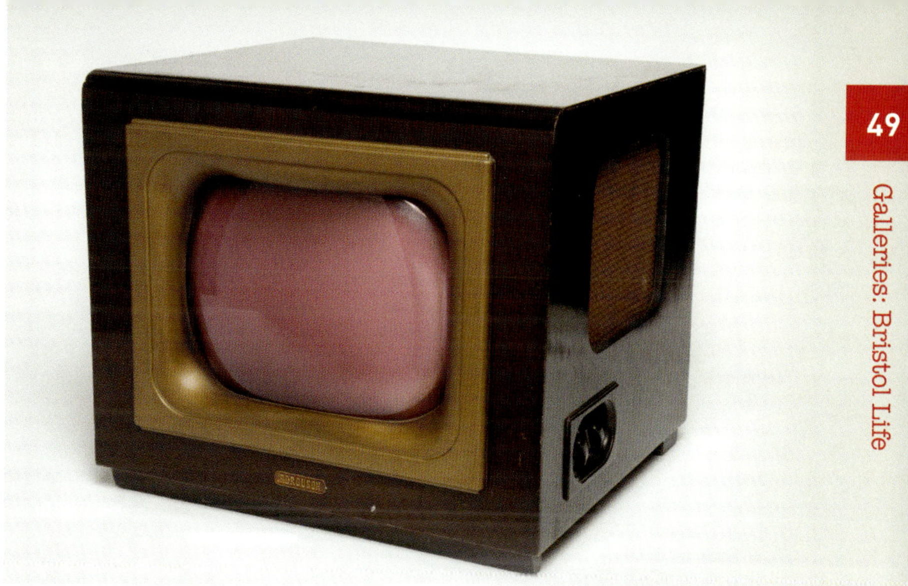

Television set, 1953, used at 16 Parson Street, Bedminster. Not everyone could afford the luxury of a TV in the 1950s. Many families bought their first TV to watch the Queen's Coronation and shared the experience with friends and neighbours.

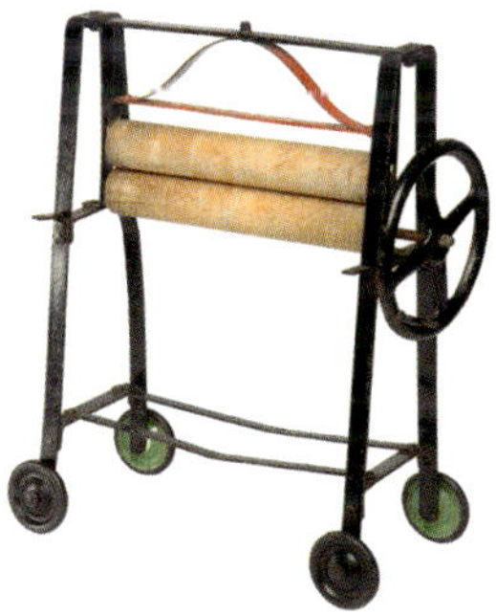

Mangles were used to squeeze water from wet washing – this toy mangle from about 1950 may have been sold as part of a set that included a clothes-horse, metal bucket, scrubbing board and pegs.

“It was very important for us always to sit down as a family and talk about our day - just to spend time together really.”

Mervyn Moors, brought up by his mother in 1950s Montpelier, Bristol.

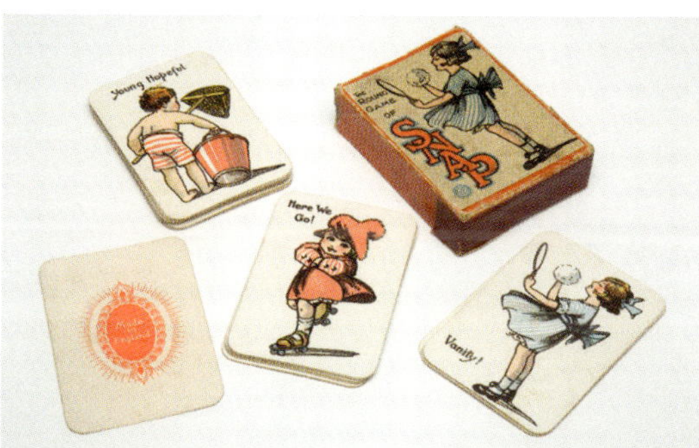

Snap playing cards, 1920s.

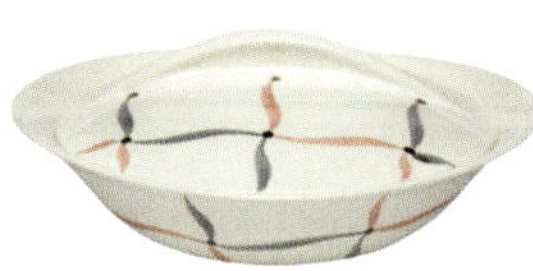

Vegetable dish from the 'Mooncurve' range, made by Pountney & Co., Ltd, Bristol in the 1950s.

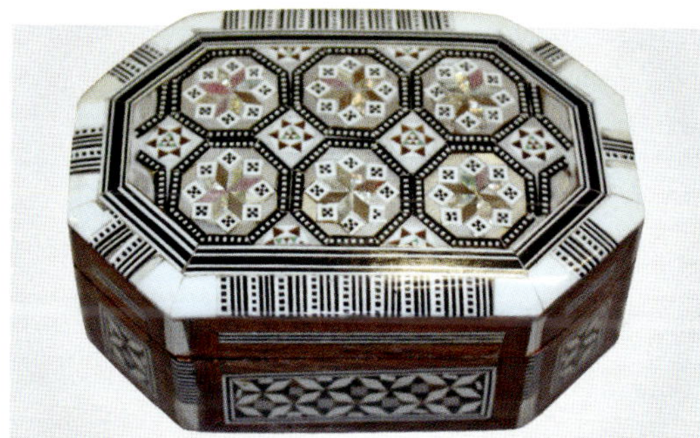

Trinket box and jewellery. This box was used by Safina Iqbal to store her jewellery which was bought in Pakistan and worn at formal occasions.

Wooden monastic bowl made in the 1400s found at Greyfriars, Bristol.

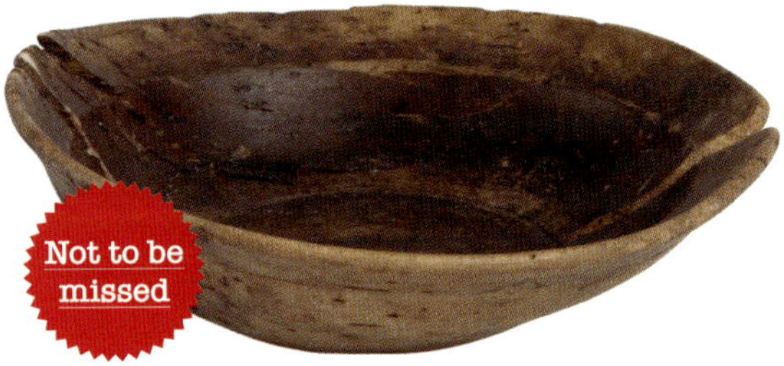

Not to be missed

Greyfriar's bowls

Not all houses are for families; religious orders also have 'houses' where people live and worship. In medieval Bristol, almost all of the religious orders were represented and a priory, abbey, nunnery and a range of friaries could all be found on the north bank of the River Frome. One of these religious houses was the Franciscan Friary in Lewin's Mead, also known as 'Greyfriars' because of the grey robes worn by the men that lived there. The friary was founded sometime before 1250. Among the finds made during excavations, that took place there in 1973, were nine complete wooden bowls and platters of all shapes and sizes, which must have been part of the domestic equipment used in the friary. These bowls are an extremely rare survival, preserved by the waterlogged conditions of the site.

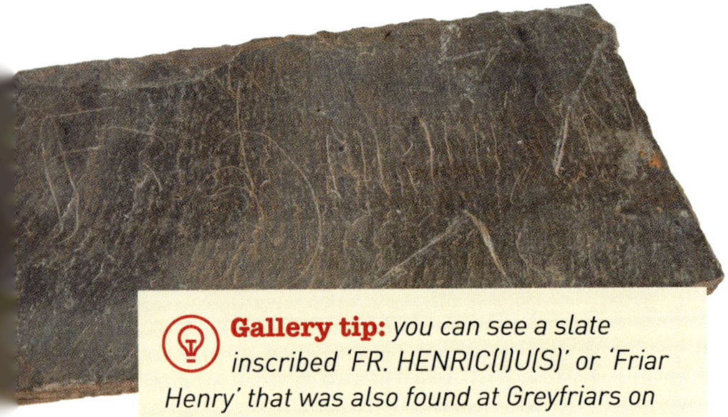

Gallery tip: *you can see a slate inscribed 'FR. HENRIC(I)U(S)' or 'Friar Henry' that was also found at Greyfriars on show in the Places Of Worship display in the Bristol Places gallery.*

Life in Müller's Orphanage

At the time of its establishment by the Reverend George Müller in 1836, the Orphan House, at Ashley Down in Bristol, was unique among contemporaries. Müller was a pioneer because orphanages at the time were so rare. Although the orphanage could not replicate family life at home, the children received an exceptional standard of care, and efforts were made to give them the happiest life possible. Ellen Petherick arrived there in 1888 with her sister and was nursed back to health. She had fond memories of living there and returned as a nurse later. Conversely, Ivy Pethick was sent to live there with her brother and sister in 1910. The children were supposed to be separated, but they were allowed to stay together. In spite of the focus on a caring environment, Ivy did not appreciate the way that she was treated while there.

Figure of Müller's Orphans, made between 1880 and 1894.

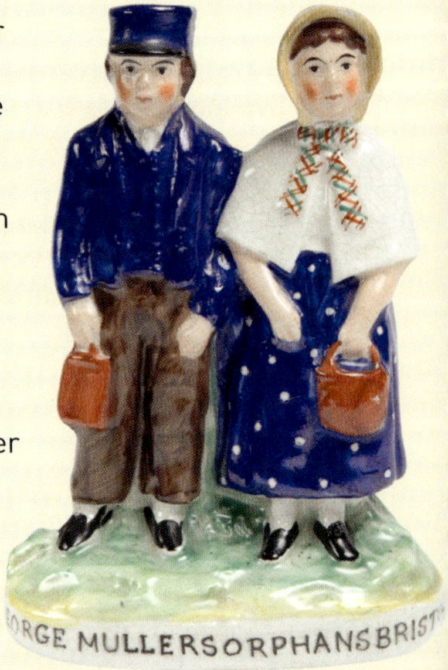

Mary Jeffries, who made this sampler, was born in 1851. The girls who lived at Müller's Orphanage made hundreds of them.

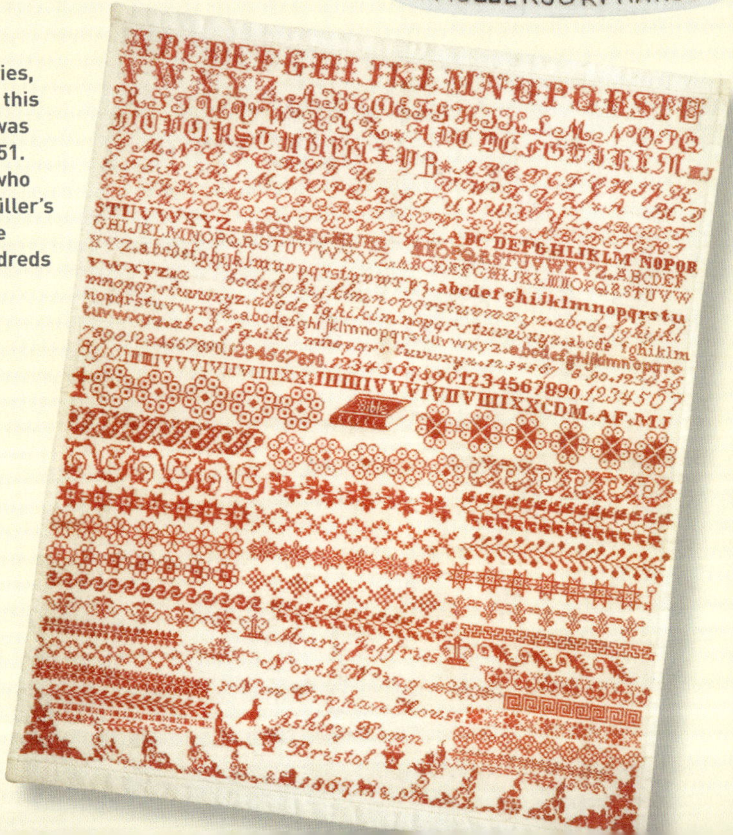

Down our street

There are many well-established and close-knit communities in Bristol and the people who live in these local neighbourhoods can either provide support to each other or be a source of local tension. The streets where people live are inextricably linked with both personal and community identity. They provide opportunities for people to connect with each other, to celebrate, to commemorate and to strengthen the ties between them.

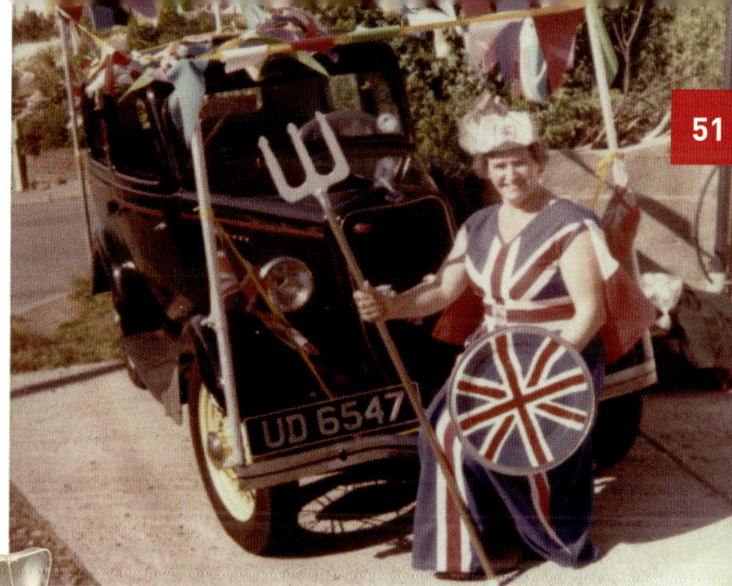

Jean Wookey made this dress to wear as part her costume for the Southmead Road street party.

Memorable moments:

Silver Jubilee street party, 1977

Many people can remember celebrating Queen Elizabeth II's Silver Jubilee in 1977. It was a time of national pride and community celebration with patriotic images and colours on display everywhere. Jean Wookey had fun celebrating it with her family and neighbours at a street party in Southmead Road, Bedminster. A huge amount of preparation was involved. Jean recalls that weeks went into its planning and that the whole street was covered in bunting. Neighbours came from adjacent streets to join in and nobody was turned away. Tables were placed along the entire length of the road and people sat down to eat a feast of sandwiches, fairy cakes, jelly and blancmange.

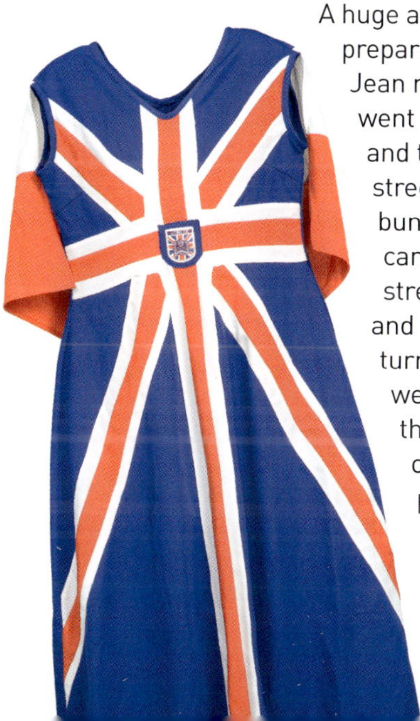

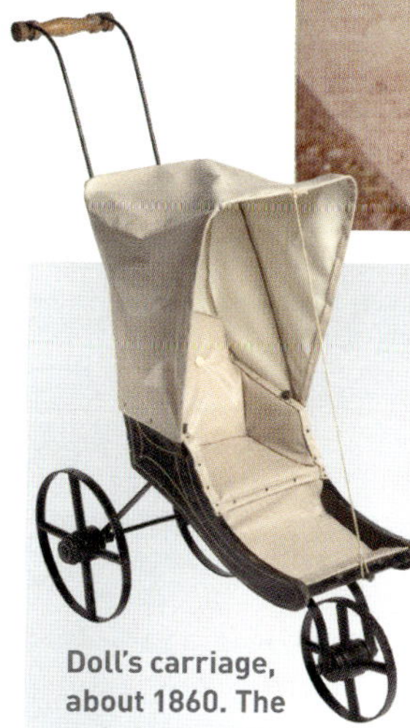

Doll's carriage, about 1860. The upholstery has been renewed.

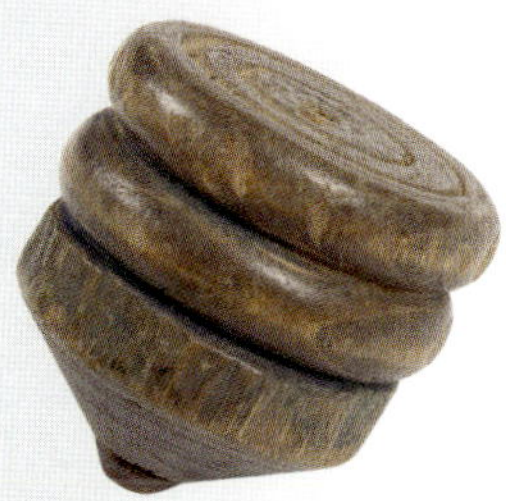

Spinning top, early 1900s.

Playing in the street

The freedom that children once had to be able to play out in the street has been curtailed by increased road traffic and fears for their safety. Alice Pickford moved to Horfield in Bristol in the 1960s and recalls that "you could play anywhere in Horfield and you wouldn't get bothered." Frank Thompson and his friends played marbles, conkers and rounders and never felt bored because when he was a child "Horfield was every child's playground." More recently however, a small parent-led action group that developed in South Bristol has now turned into national movement to help children play out. By 2018 'Playing Out' had helped children to enjoy playing in over 660 streets spread across 67 local authority areas.

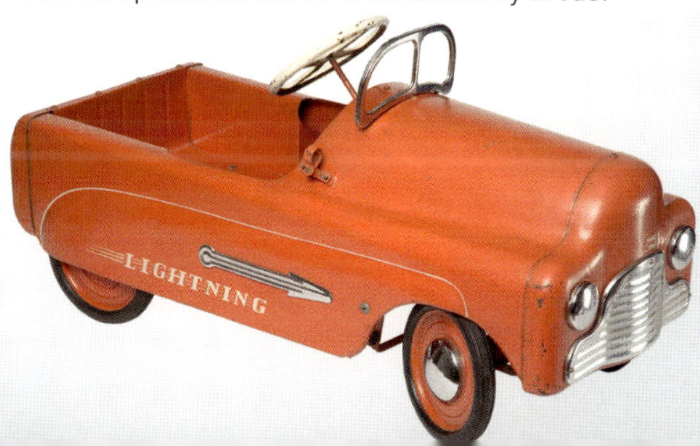

Pedal car, 1950s. Martin of Coaley Road, Shirehampton, received this car for his first birthday in 1952.

Learning places

Over time, whether adult or child, there have been increasing numbers of opportunities provided for people to be able to learn in the city. The experiences they share and the relationships they develop often stand out in their memories. From inspirational teaching to stink bombs in the playground, for some they can be the worst of or the best of times.

Alfred goes missing

Bristol's students, like many others around the country, have enjoyed a long tradition of both mischief-making and fundraising during their annual 'Rag week'. This is a week when students traditionally carry out unusual stunts to raise money for charity. In 1956, in a bid to execute a particularly daring Rag week prank, three students from Bristol caused uproar when they kidnapped the stuffed body of Alfred the gorilla from Bristol Museum. Alfred was photographed with his kidnappers and then returned. The students involved kept their identities secret for over 50 years.

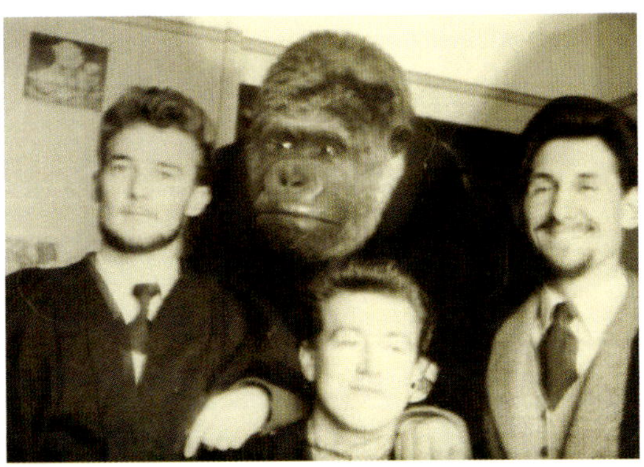

Left to right: DB, Alfred the gorilla, Fred Hooper and Ron Morgan during Alfred's Rag week disappearance in 1956. © Fred Hooper and Ron Morgan

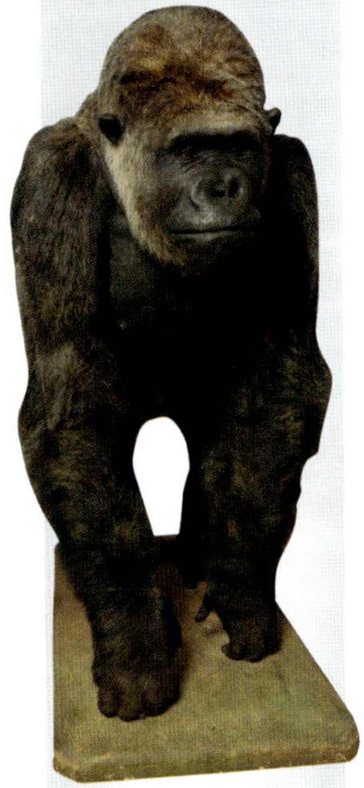

Alfred the gorilla at Bristol Museum. It's hard to understand how the students managed to cram him into the back of a Vauxhall car to make their getaway!

Did you know?

Bristol's Red Maids' school was founded in 1634 from the bequest of John Whitson, Mayor and MP of Bristol, making it the oldest surviving girls' school in England.

Not to be missed

Industrial school doll, late 1800s-early 1900s

This doll is dressed in the uniform of the Clifton Industrial School for Boys in Bristol. Pupils at such schools made uniforms for dolls that were then sold to raise money for the school. The Clifton Industrial School was established in 1849 in Pennywell Road and later moved to larger premises in Clifton Wood. Industrial schools were intended to help children who were destitute. In 1857, the Industrial Schools Act gave magistrates the power to sentence children aged between 7-14 years old to spend time in one of these institutions if they had been brought before the courts for vagrancy (homelessness). In 1861, a further act was passed that covered other categories of children, for example, those under 14s who had been found begging or whose parents declared them beyond control.

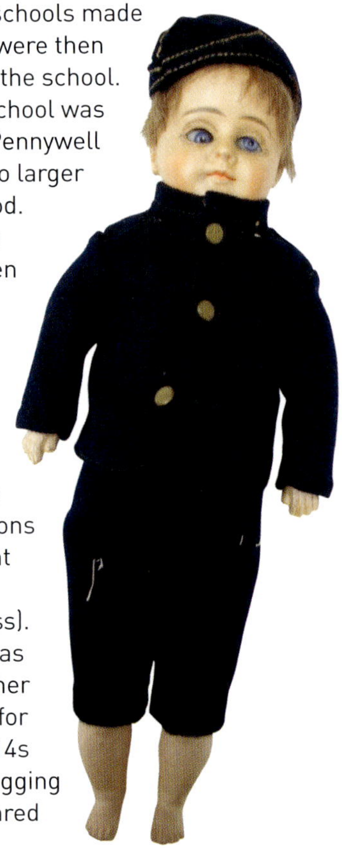

Mary Carpenter's 'Ragged School'

Mary Carpenter set up her Ragged School in 1846. The pupils came from very deprived backgrounds. They wore tattered and filthy clothes, and were ill-disciplined. Gradually, however, the boys began to enjoy their lessons with Mary, but continued to interrupt them by playing games, whistling or fighting.

At work

Since many people spend a good deal of their waking hours at work it goes without saying that they may develop strong relationships with their co-workers and managers. Bristol people have had, and continue to have, a wide variety of occupations. Some have been exploited, some have made a stand, and some are unacknowledged, but they have all influenced the life and identity of the city.

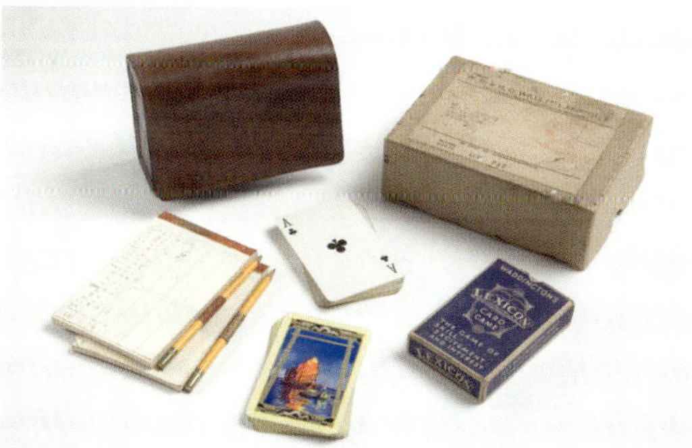

Wills' had a reputation as a considerate employer, giving gifts to long-standing and retiring members of staff, like this playing card compendium.

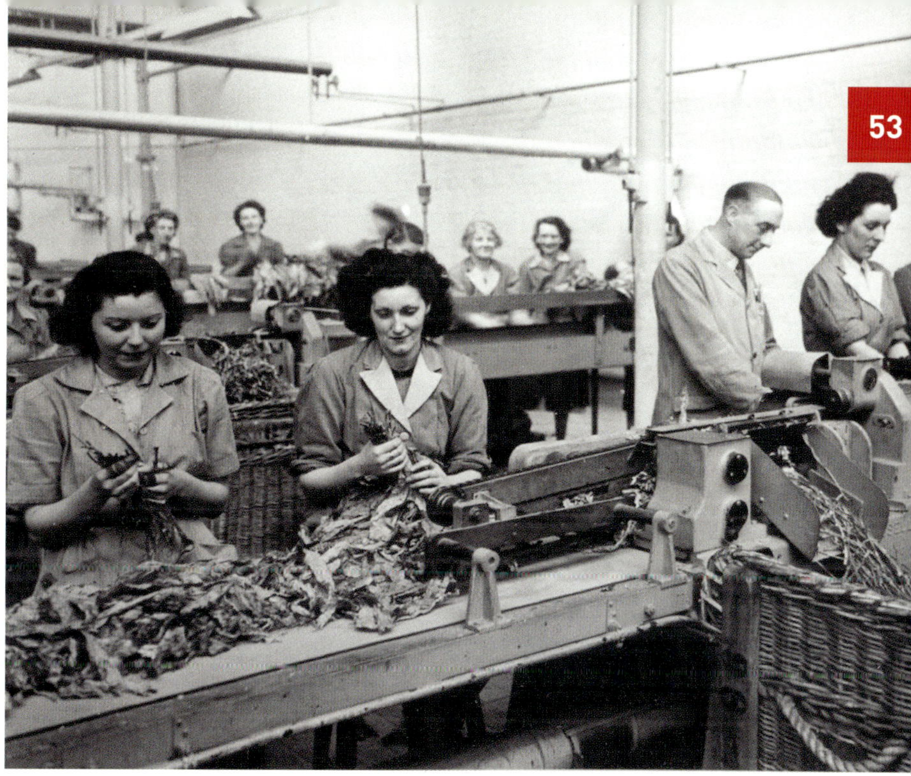

Photograph of staff at work stripping tobacco leaves for cigar making at W.D. & H.O. Wills' factory, Bristol, about 1950. © Imperial Tobacco Ltd, England

Working at Wills' tobacco factories

From the end of the 1800s, and through most of the 1900s, tobacco production was one of the foremost industries in Bristol. The industry centred on the Wills' factories in Bedminster, where the workforce was largely female and local. Work was hard and often mundane, but the relationships forged by the workers and the social facilities provided by the company led to many workers remembering their days at Wills' as happy ones. Many of Wills' workers came from the close-knit communities surrounding the factories and counted family members among their colleagues. Their social relationships were important and often long lasting, but office staff and factory people were not encouraged to mix.

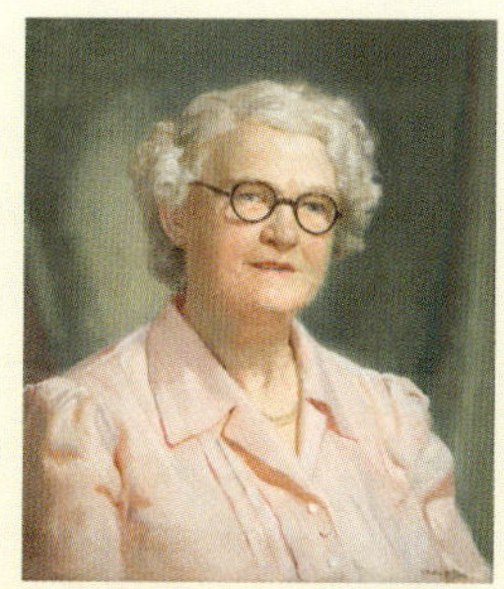

© The artist's estate

Miss Ellen Williams, about 1952 by Arthur Wilson Gay (1901-1958)

Ellen worked at Wills' from 1906 to 1952 in the No 1 Factory Stemming Room. She was a member of the No 1 Factory Council. During World War II her work included sending cigarettes from Wills' factories to the Armed Forces.

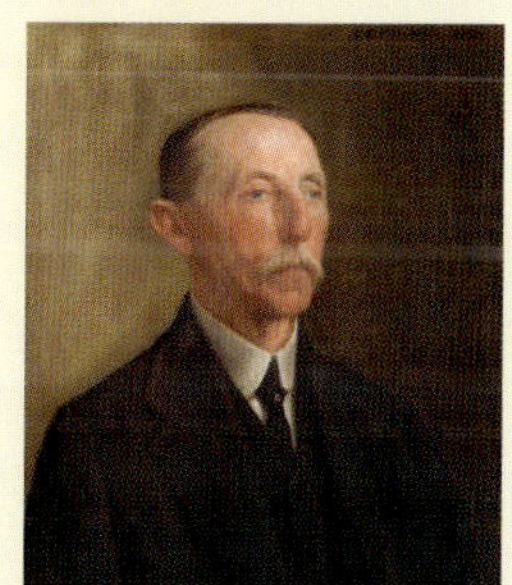

© The artist's estate

Mr William Masters Davies, 1920 by Reginald Edgar James Bush (1869-1956)

This portrait was painted to mark William Davies' 40th year of service. He worked at Wills' from 1879 to 1928. William started in the Invoice Office, became Head of the Department in 1888, and by 1900 was Head of the Stores.

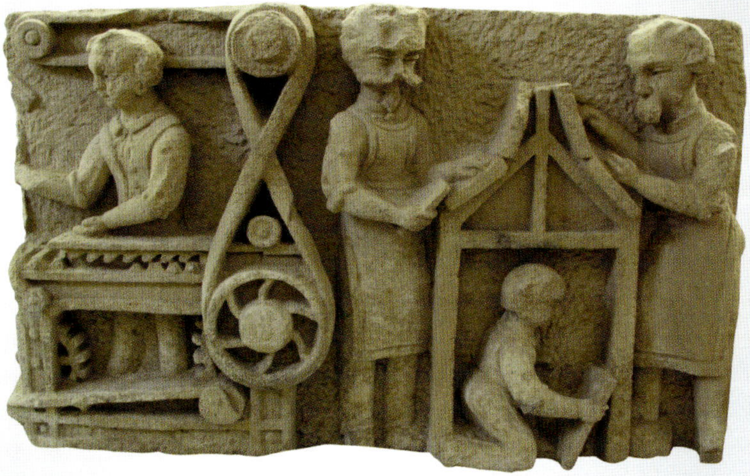

Apprentices

From the medieval period right up until the 1900s, entry into skilled trades could only be gained by the system of apprenticeship. Under this system an apprentice would exchange labour for training, food and accommodation. While the contracts or 'indentures' governing apprenticeships were legally binding documents, the system was open to abuse. Court records show many instances of apprentices bringing grievances against their masters and vice versa. For example in 1785, George Anstice was apprenticed to James Perry, a cordwainer (shoemaker). George accused his master of mistreatment and not instructing him in a trade.

Robinson factory frieze (replica). When brothers Elisha and Alfred Robinson built a new factory in Redcliff Street in the 1870s, they commissioned a frieze showing different activities associated with the packaging works. This replica, made in 2010, is of one of the 15 sections, which shows an apprentice working with typesetters.

Did you know?

Elisha Robinson hit on the idea of producing wrappers and bags printed with the name of the shop and a design from a huge stock of pictures. When a bag making machine was invented in America, Robinson bought the rights to manufacture it in Britain. His business grew into DRG, one of the giants of the packaging industry in the UK.

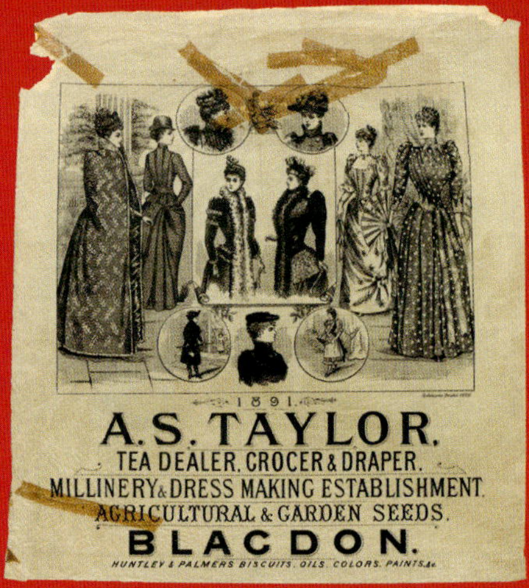

Gallery tip: *you can see products of Bristol's paper bag-making industry in the Bristol People gallery.*

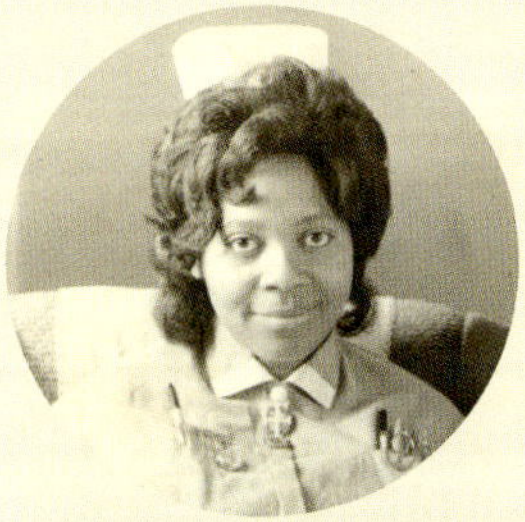

Photograph of Princess Campbell in uniform, 1960s. Given by Dennis Perry. Bristol Archives 43846/1

Princess Campbell MBE (1939-2015)

Princess Campbell came to Bristol from Jamaica in 1962 and applied to Wills' tobacco factory for a job. She became the first Black person to work there. After two years Princess decided she wanted to train as an NHS nurse. There were few job opportunities for African-Caribbean people and she remembers that black nurses 'got the worst jobs and the worst shifts.' Princess realised that, to gain promotion, she would have to work harder and earn more qualifications than her white colleagues. Through her determination and drive, she was appointed ward sister at Glenside Psychiatric Hospital, where she completed many years of distinguished service, setting high standards in nursing care until she retired in the 1990s. Throughout her life she campaigned tirelessly on behalf of disadvantaged communities and, in 2011, she received an MBE for services to the community in the Queen's Birthday Honours list.

In the city

Bristol is a vibrant hub of social and cultural activity with a wide variety of city-based events for its people and visitors to enjoy in their spare time. There's something to suit everyone's taste, whether that be for music, street art, food, sporting or outdoor fun. However, as you'll discover, what was considered to be entertaining in the past might raise a few eyebrows today.

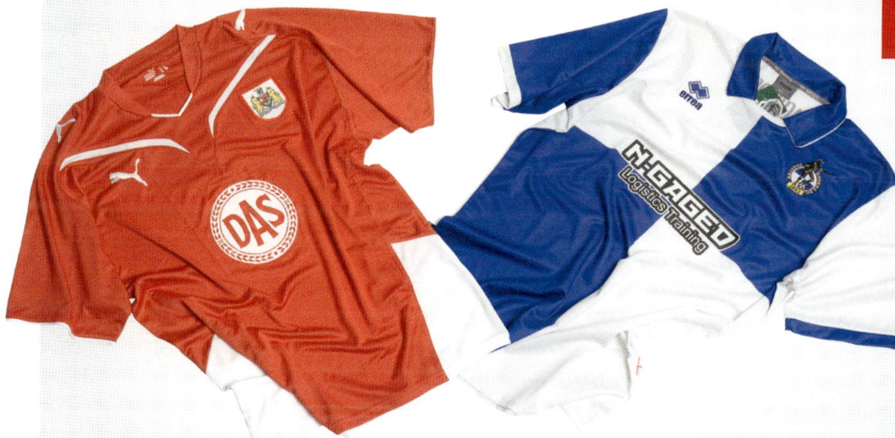

Are you a 'Red' or a 'Blue'? Replica Bristol City and Bristol Rovers football shirts, (2009-10).

Sporting city

It's hard to believe that little more than 120 years ago Bristol had almost no purpose-built stadia for mass spectator sports. The lack of stadia did not mean that organised sport wasn't a feature in Bristol at all; areas such as the Downs were home to a wide variety of sporting activities from the 1800s onwards. A plethora of local clubs grew up, formed around social networks related to chapels and churches, lads' brigades, factories and specific localities. From greyhound to speedway racing, from bowls to football, rugby and cricket, there's always been a sport of one kind or another for Bristol's people to pledge their allegiance to.

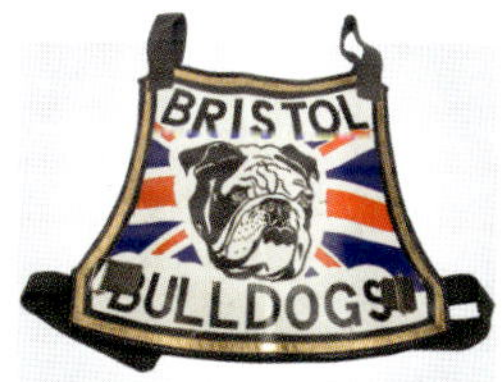

Bristol Bulldogs racing bib. The Bristol Bulldogs was a motorcycle speedway team formed prior to World War II. They raced at the now-demolished Knowle Stadium.

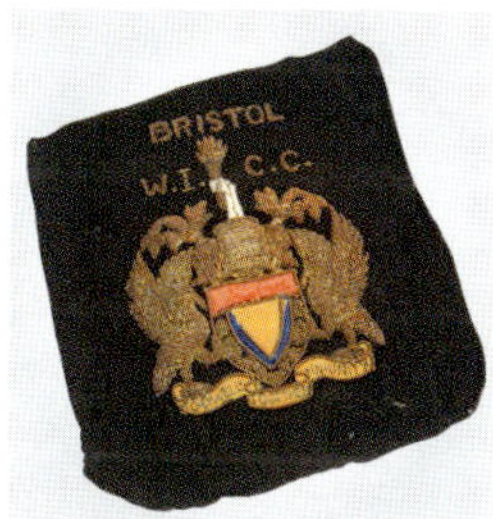

Bristol West Indian Cricket Club blazer badge. Bristol WICC 'Dwell Together in Unity'.

Bristol Archives 43745/5/5

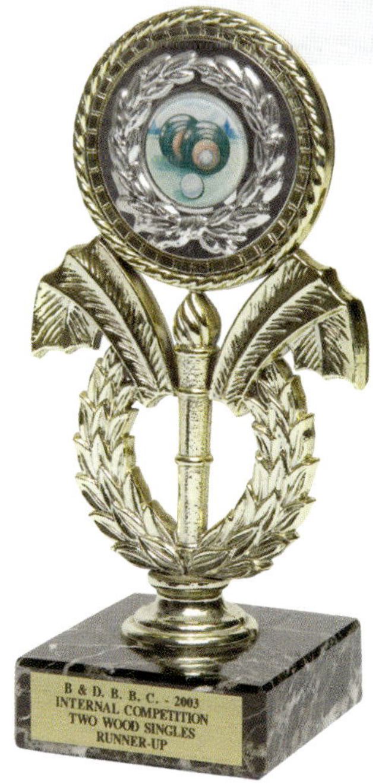

Trophy: Bristol & District Blind Bowling Club. 2003.

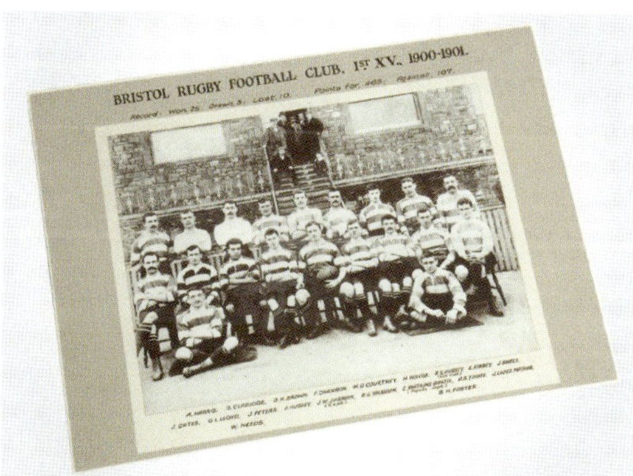

A photograph of Bristol Rugby Football Club 1st XV, 1900–1901 season. It includes Jimmy Peters, England's first black international rugby player.

Bristol Archives 41582/IM/Ph/1/12

Did you know?

Durdham Down in Bristol was used for horse-racing during the 1800s. A painting by artist Rolinda Sharples (1793-1838), which depicts the races in 1836, can be seen in the Bristol Places gallery.

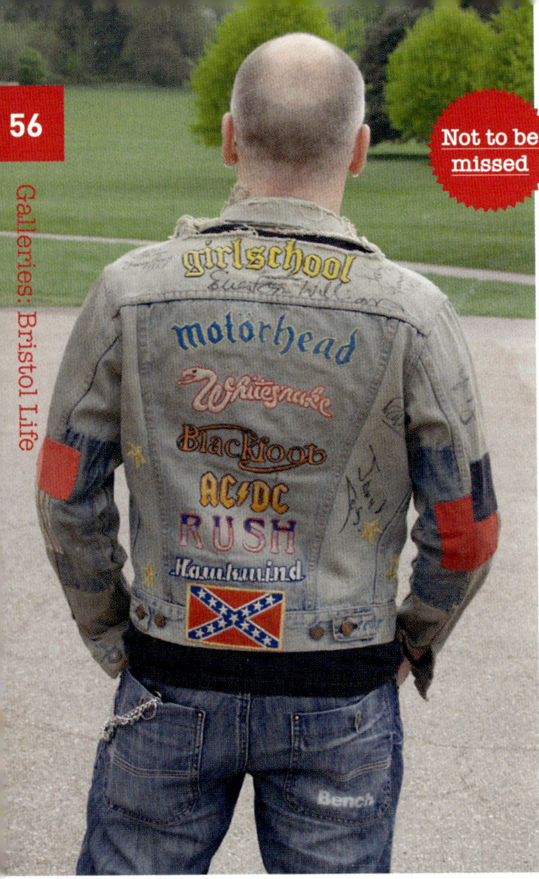

Not to be missed

Denim jacket, about 1980

Jonathon Kardasz wore this jacket to the Heavy Metal concerts he began to attend in Bristol during the 1980s. He saw many bands perform including Iron Maiden, Judas Priest and Motorhead. The jacket has been decorated with the names of Heavy Metal bands and is deliberately soiled and torn. Jonathon recalls that wearing a jacket like this "would mark you out to friends or foes. It helped express our solidarity with other metal fans." Jonathon embroidered the logos of his favourite bands onto the jacket himself. The more obscure the band emblazoned on a jacket like this the better, as it would signal a true devotion and interest in the scene. One of the badges is a Confederate flag. Jonathon says he put it there "simply because of its association with Southern Rock and particularly Lynyrd Skynyrd... in those days it certainly didn't have the same highly charged connotations as it does now, at least in the UK, and it simply represented a style of music and a naive idea of what constituted a 'rebel'. Would I keep it on the jacket if I was wearing it now? Of course not."

A selection of tickets collected by Jonathon Kardasz since 1980 for concerts at Bristol venues such as the Thekla, the Bierkeller and the Colston Hall.

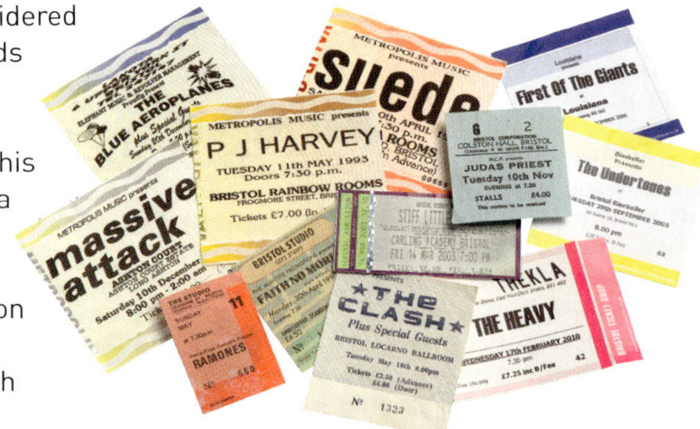

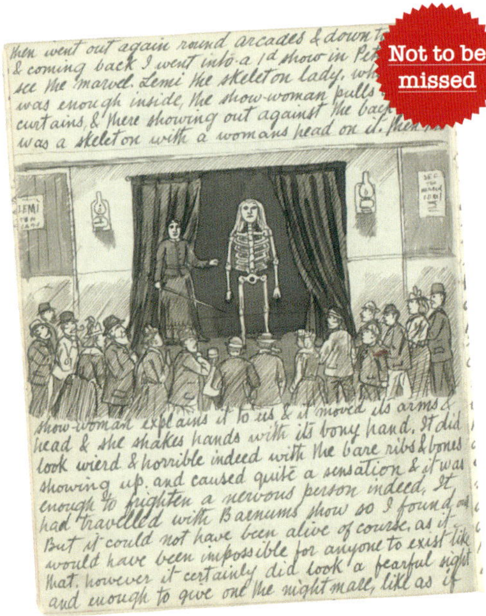

Not to be missed

The diary of Harry Bow

William Henry Bow, known as Harry, was born in Bristol in 1865. He worked as a pallbearer, helping to carry coffins at funerals, but he also kept highly detailed and illustrated diaries observing life in the late 1800s. Travelling shows and circuses were a popular form of entertainment at that time and they would typically feature individuals with medically extreme or impossible medical conditions, who were presented to an eager crowd waiting to be astonished or horrified. An atmosphere of anticipation was created by a master showman, or woman in this case, who would stand outside the entrance and explain what bizarre sights could be seen on payment of an entry fee.

This extract from Harry Bow's diary describes a visit to a travelling show on Peter Street, 8 August 1891. The crowd was shocked to see 'Lemi the skeleton lady'. A curtain was drawn back to reveal a 'weird and horrible' skeleton with a woman's head.

And finally...

take in the ever-changing view of the city by spending time looking through M Shed's dedicated 'Window on Bristol'.

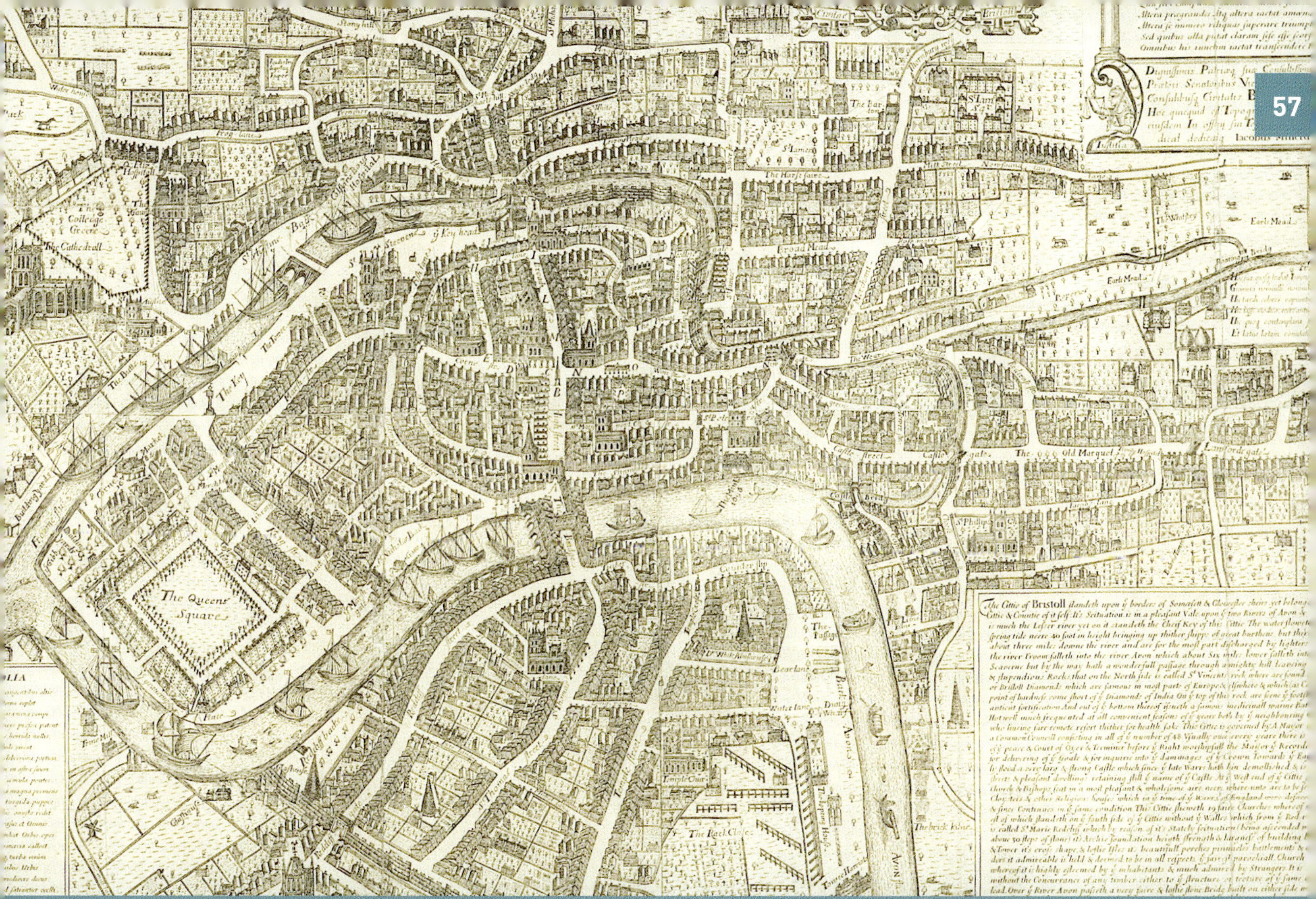

James Millerd's *Exact Delineation of the Famous City of Bristoll* of 1673. This was the first detailed map of Bristol and records many landmarks that can still be seen today.
Bristol Archives 31416/1

Reproduction copies of some of Bristol's historic maps are available to buy in the museum shop.

Bristol Destinations

M Shed sits at the heart of the city with plenty of places that can be explored and enjoyed within easy walking distance.

Out and about in Bristol...

Bristol's natural landscape, its architectural, maritime and industrial heritage, and the actions and activities of its people, have all left, and continue to leave, their mark on the city. It has been home to world-famous explorers, artists and poets, scientists, inventors and engineers as well as religious and political reformers. Their stories and those of the people that live here today are behind many of the city's familiar and unfamiliar landmarks.

Bristol's appearance is constantly changing as new shops, offices and houses are built and old ones demolished. Sometimes the only evidence we have of what the city used to look like comes from drawings and paintings like this one of Broad Street in about 1824 by Edward Cashin.

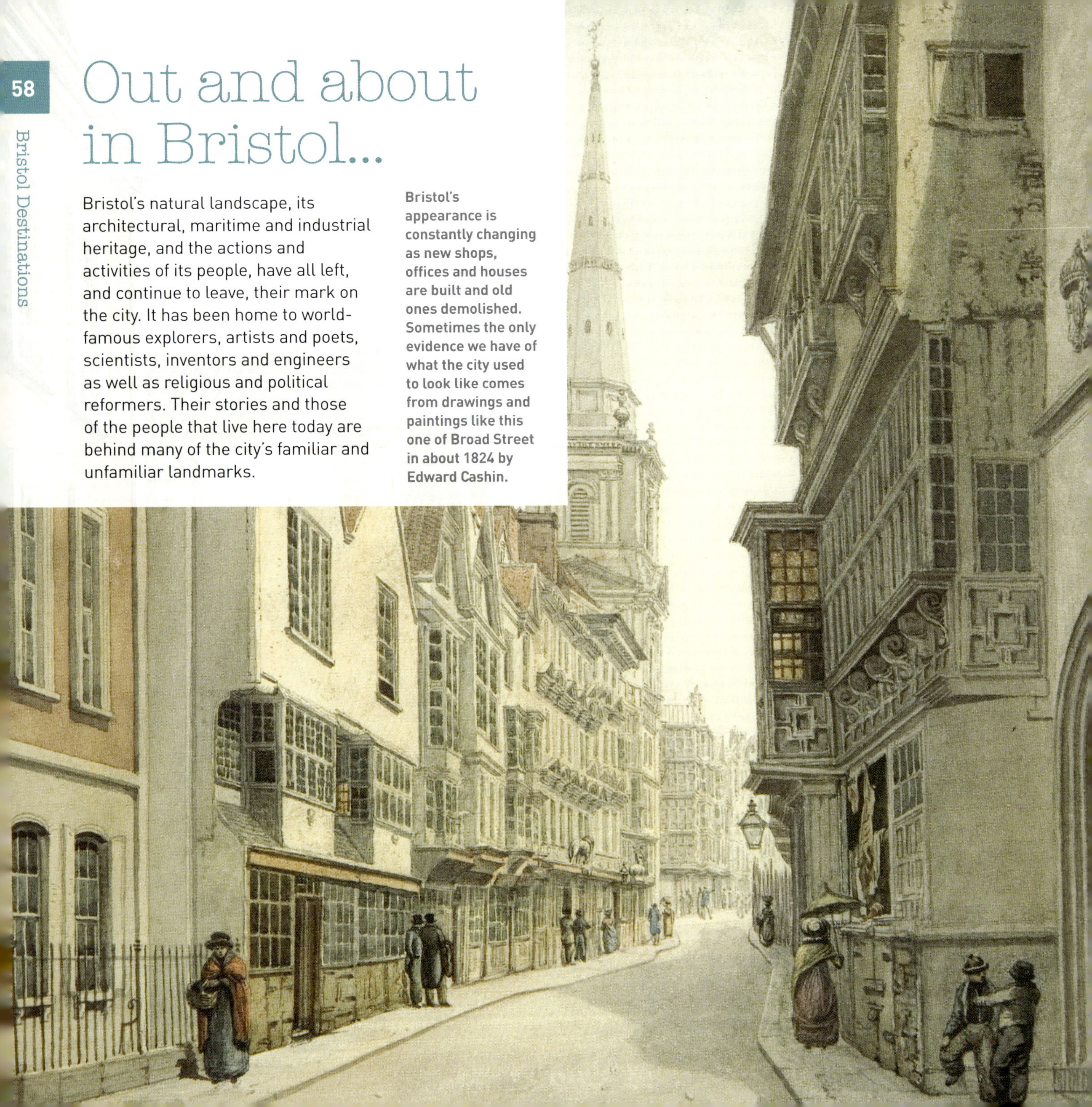

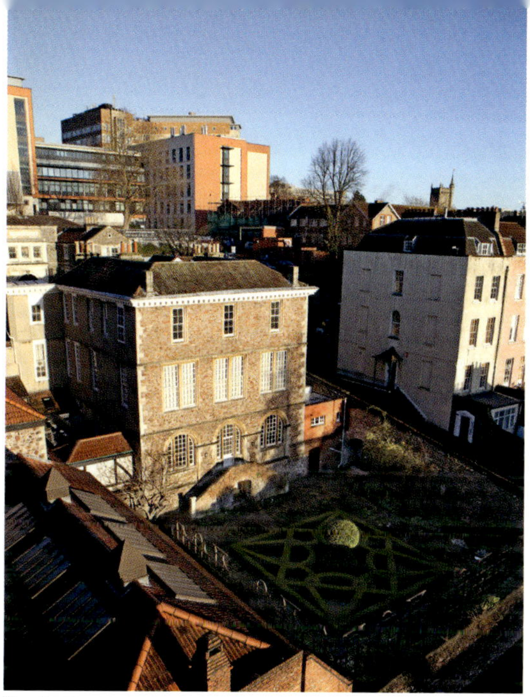

© zedphoto.com

The Red Lodge Museum

One of Bristol's hidden gems, this is a Tudor building, with original interiors, a knot garden and a captivating 400 year history. The original Elizabethan lodge is made up of three rooms which show it as it was in 1580. The Great Oak Room is the last complete room of this period in Bristol.

Elizabethan splendour

Inside the Red Lodge, the Great Oak Room is decorated with wooden panelling, an elaborate plaster ceiling and impressive stone fireplace showing exotic motifs of the age.

Park Row, Bristol BS1

5LJ: 0.7 miles - 16 minutes

The Red Lodge was an addition to John Young's Great House – find out more in the Bristol Places Gallery: Places to Live & Enjoy

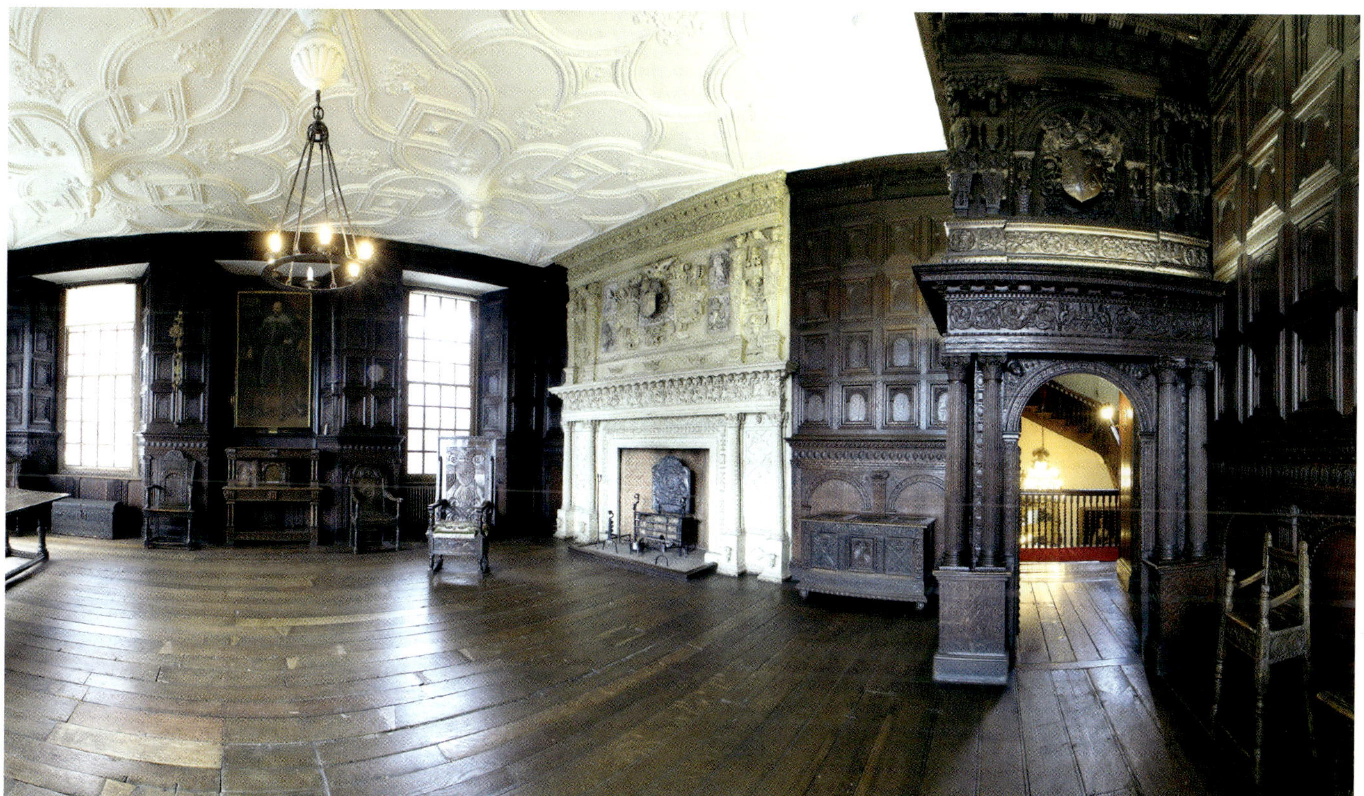

© zedphoto.com

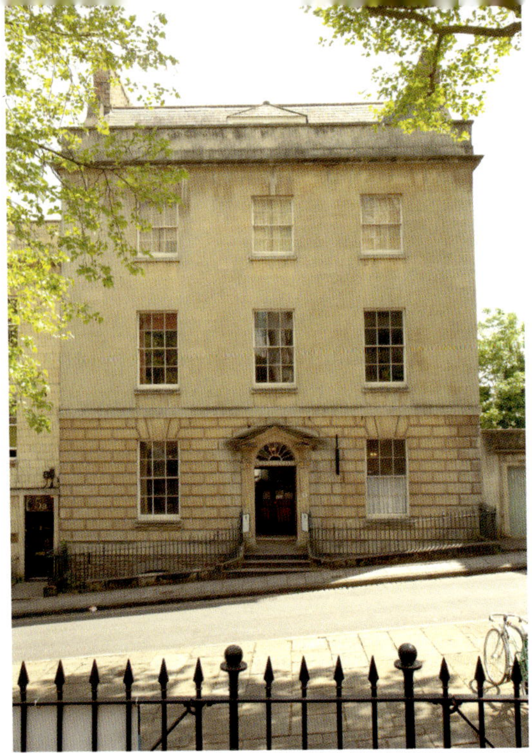

The Georgian House Museum

This restored 1790 townhouse offers a fascinating insight into life above and below stairs. The house was built for John Pinney, slave plantation owner and sugar merchant. A small display explores Pinney's involvement in the sugar trade and the life of his enslaved valet, Pero Jones, who was of African descent.

7 Great George Street, Bristol BS1
5RR: 0.7 miles - 16 minutes

Bristol's involvement in the Transatlantic Slave Trade is explored in more detail in the Bristol People Gallery.

Georgian House kitchen

Step back in time and experience the elegance of this Georgian townhouse complete with dining room, drawing room, study and even a cold plunge pool.

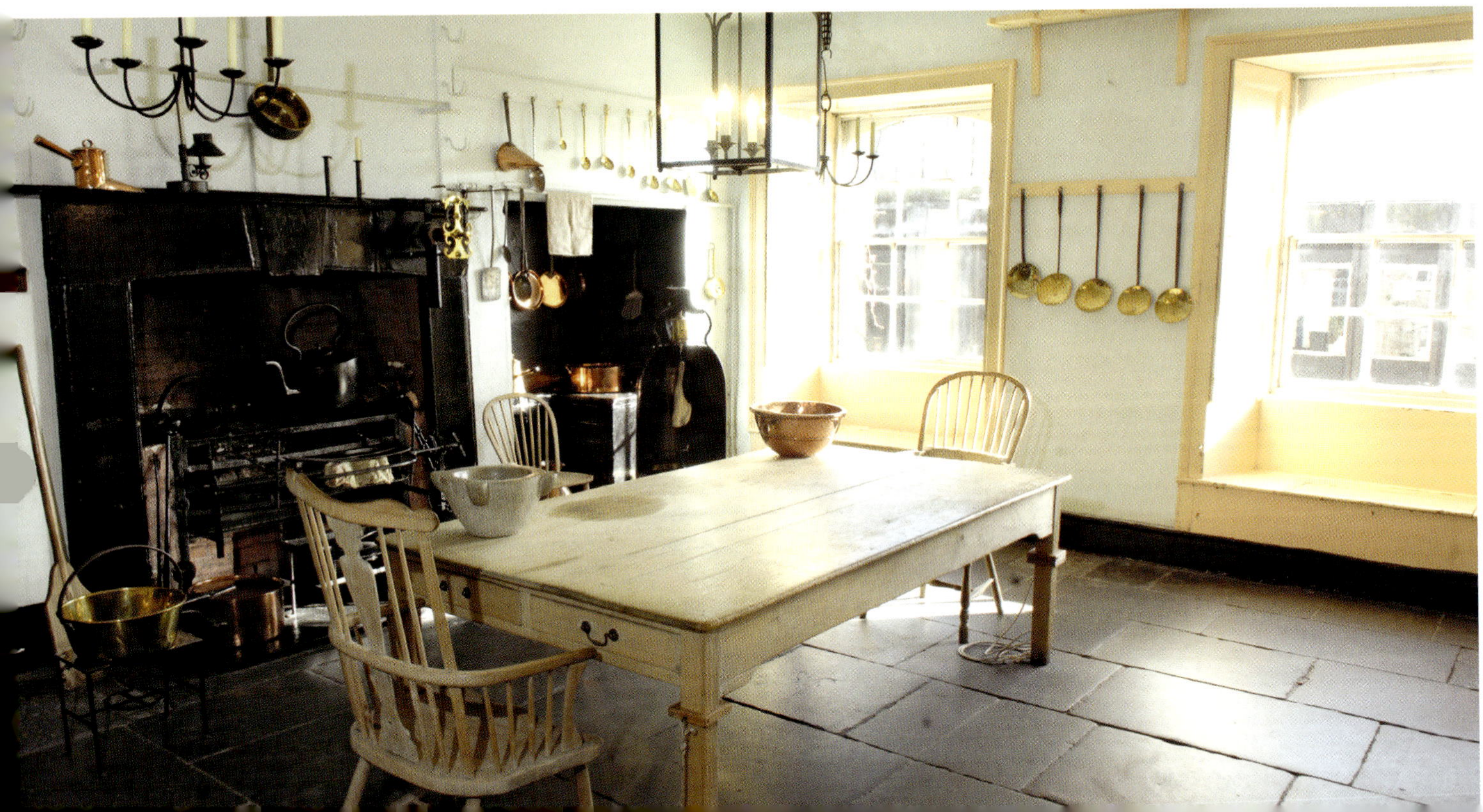

Bristol Museum & Art Gallery

This beautiful Edwardian building was gifted to the city by Sir William Henry Wills and designed by his cousin, Sir Frank William Wills. It opened in 1905 as the Art Gallery and Museum of Antiquities but now houses world-class collections of the natural world, art, archaeology and world cultures.

Queens Road, Bristol BS8 1RL:
0.8 miles - 20 minutes

Sir Frank William Wills also designed the Wills tobacco factory building at East Street in Bedminster. Find out more in the Bristol Places Gallery: Places to Work and the Bristol Life Gallery: At Work.

The Bristol Boxkite in Bristol Museum & Art Gallery

Hanging up high in the front hall is a full scale near replica of the Bristol Biplane or 'Boxkite'. No original boxkites have survived anywhere. This example is one of three built from the original drawings by Miles and Co. for the 1964 film 'Those Magnificent Men in Their Flying Machines', where it featured as the Phoenix Flyer.

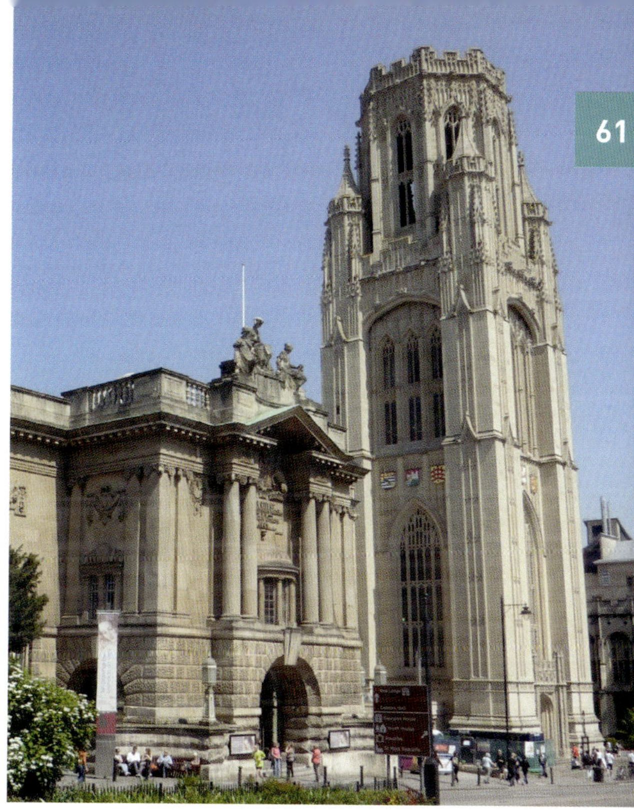

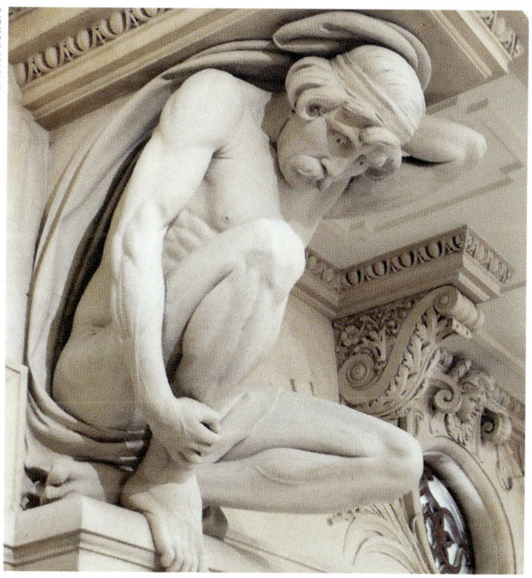

Inside Bristol Museum & Art Gallery

Sculpted figures and architectural detail fill the inside of Bristol Museum & Art Gallery – what will you find?

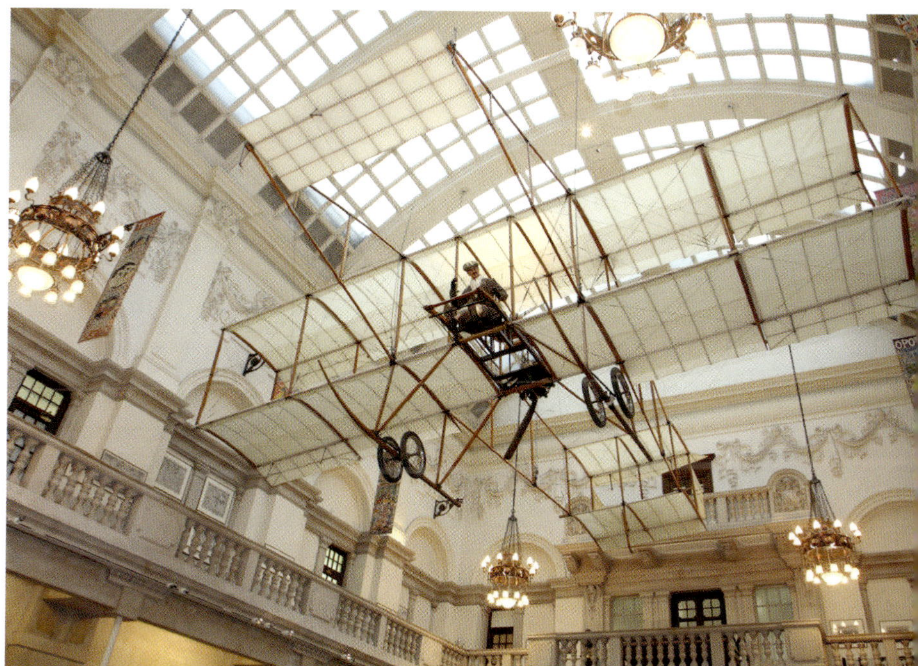

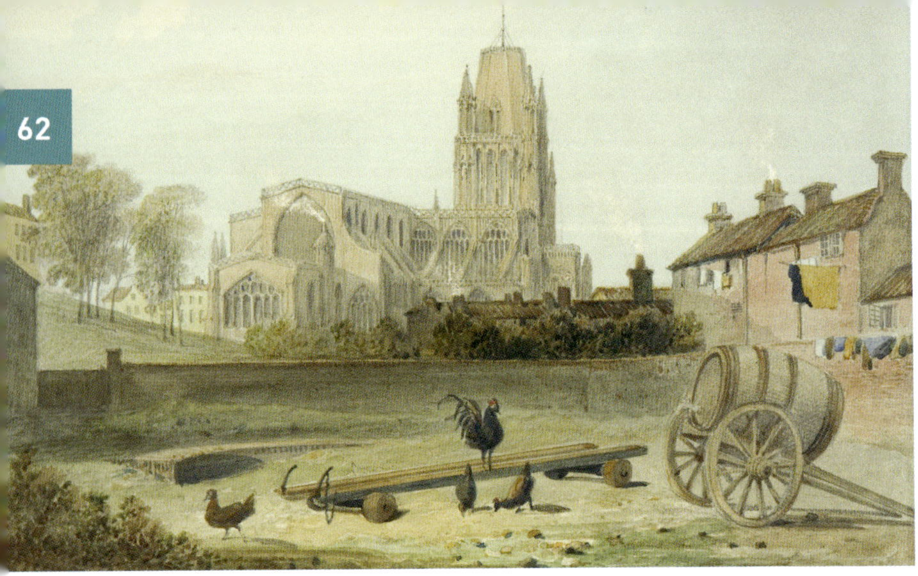

St Mary Redcliffe

The parish church of St Mary Redcliffe has been a place of Christian worship for over 900 years. It is renowned for the beauty of its architecture. Its original spire was destroyed by lightning in 1446 and was eventually restored in 1872. The church also contains many monuments to individuals who lived and worked in the city.

Redcliffe Way, Bristol:
0.5 miles – 10 minutes
Some of Bristol's most iconic and long-lived buildings are places of worship relating to many different faiths. Find out more in the Bristol Places Gallery: Places of Worship, Education & Control.

St Mary Redcliffe
St Mary Redcliffe as it appeared without its spire in a painting called St Mary Redcliffe Church from the north-east by Thomas Leeson Rowbotham (1782-1853).

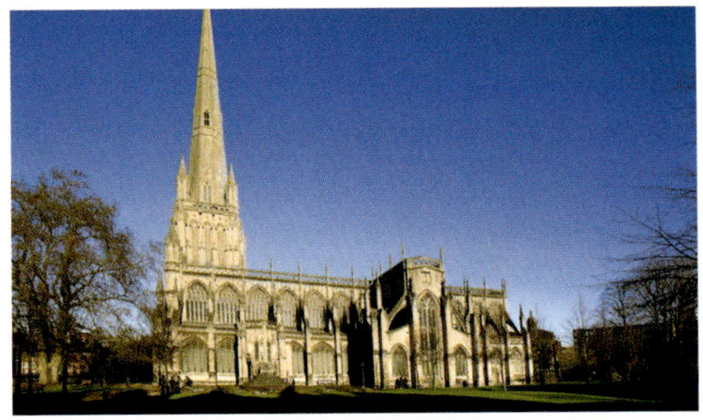

© zedphoto.com

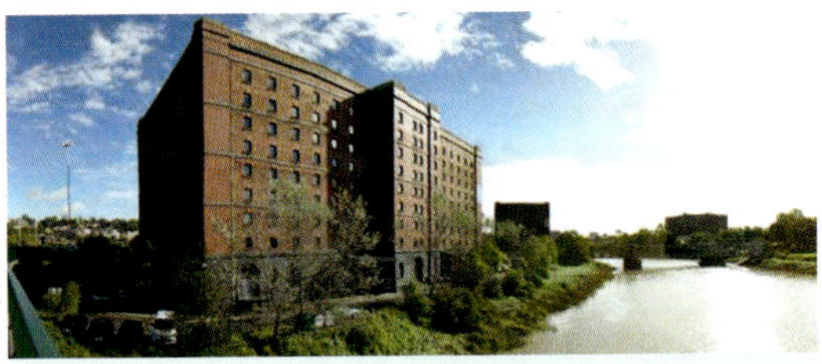

© zedphoto.com

Smeaton Road, Cumberland Basin Bristol BS1 6XN:
1.2 miles - 23 minutes
Many of the original documents and images on show at M Shed belong to the Bristol Archives' collection. The oldest document, called the 'Charter of Theobald', is on show in Bristol Places Gallery: Places of Worship, Education & Control.

Bristol Archives

A former bonded warehouse built to serve Bristol's harbour in 1908 is now the home to over 850 years of Bristol's history, from documents and deeds to photographs, letters and diaries, film and sound recordings. Known as 'B' bond, it was one of three warehouses constructed to service the tobacco import business in the early 1900s.

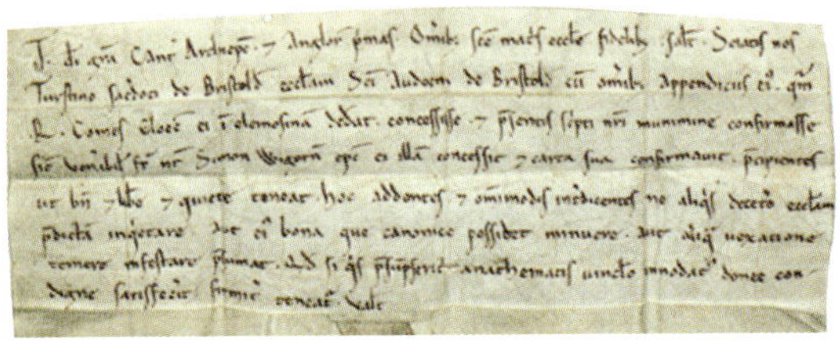

Charter of Theobald, 1140s
Theobald, Archbishop of Canterbury, issued this charter to confirm Turstin of Bristol as priest of St Ewen, one of Bristol's earliest churches. Theobald threatened anyone who might interfere with damnation and so the charter became known as the 'Curse of St Ewen'.

Bristol Archives P.St E/A/1

Brandon Hill

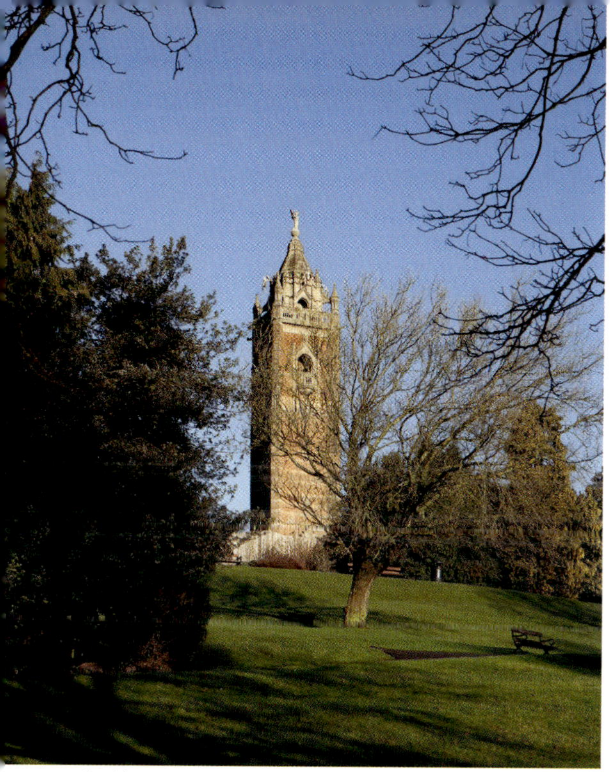

© zedphoto.com

Since 1625, Brandon Hill has been used for 'unrestricted recreational pursuits' making it one of the country's oldest public open spaces. During the English Civil War (1642-46) the hill became part of the city's outer defences and some of the earthworks associated with these still survive. It was used for grazing until 1670 and then for hay-making, clothes-drying and carpet-beating. Today it is a popular city-centre park with excellent views.

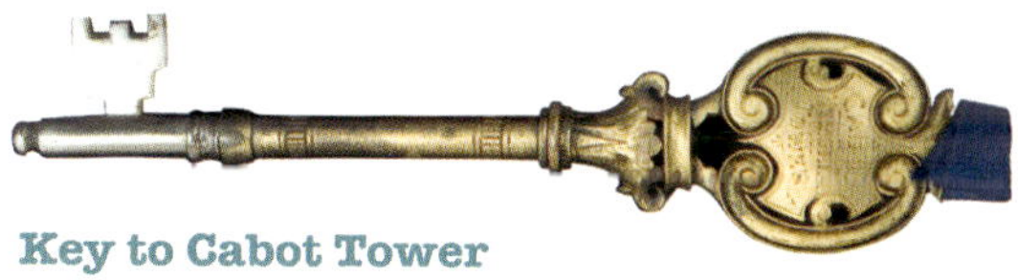

Key to Cabot Tower
Cabot Tower is open to the public and free to visit. Climb to the top for panoramic views across the city.

Bristol Archives 01276

Cabot Tower, Bristol BS8 1HJ: 0.9 miles – 18 minutes
Cabot Tower was built between 1896 and 1898 to mark the 400th anniversary of John Cabot's voyage of exploration from Bristol to America. You can see the key used at the opening ceremony in the Bristol Places Gallery: Open Spaces.

Queen Square

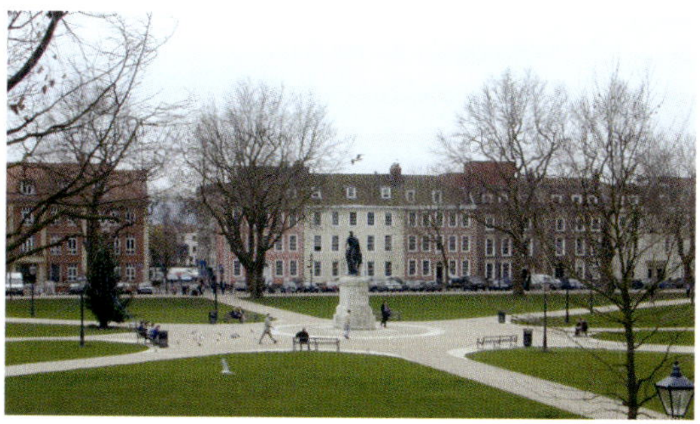

© Bristol City Council

Queen Square was a fashionable development outside the city walls in the early 1700s. It was designed to be one of the largest and grandest residential squares in Europe. Occupied by rich merchants, and at one time, the home of the first overseas US Consulate, it was the main location for the riots of 1831.

Queen Square, Bristol BS1 4LH: 0.3 miles – 5 minutes
Learn more about the development of Queen Square in the Bristol Places Gallery: Places to Live & Enjoy and about the 1831 riots in the Bristol People Gallery: Challenging.

Queen Square from above
Before Queen Square was built it was known as the Town Marsh and was a popular place for recreation. After the 1831 riots caused the destruction of half of the houses on the square it fell into decline. It was restored to its 1817 layout in the late 1990s.

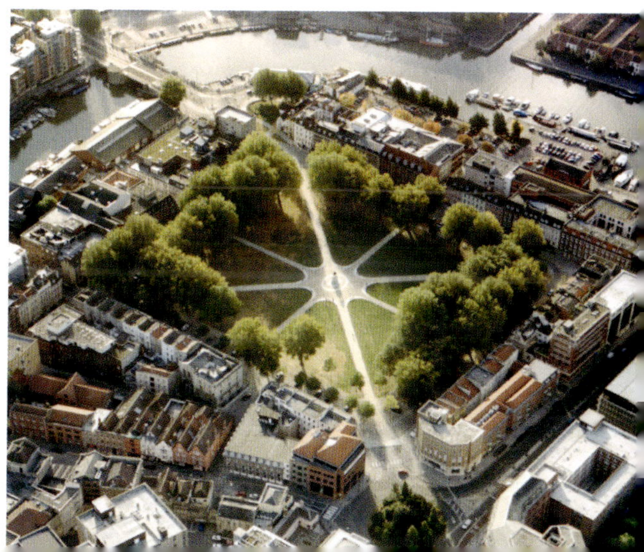

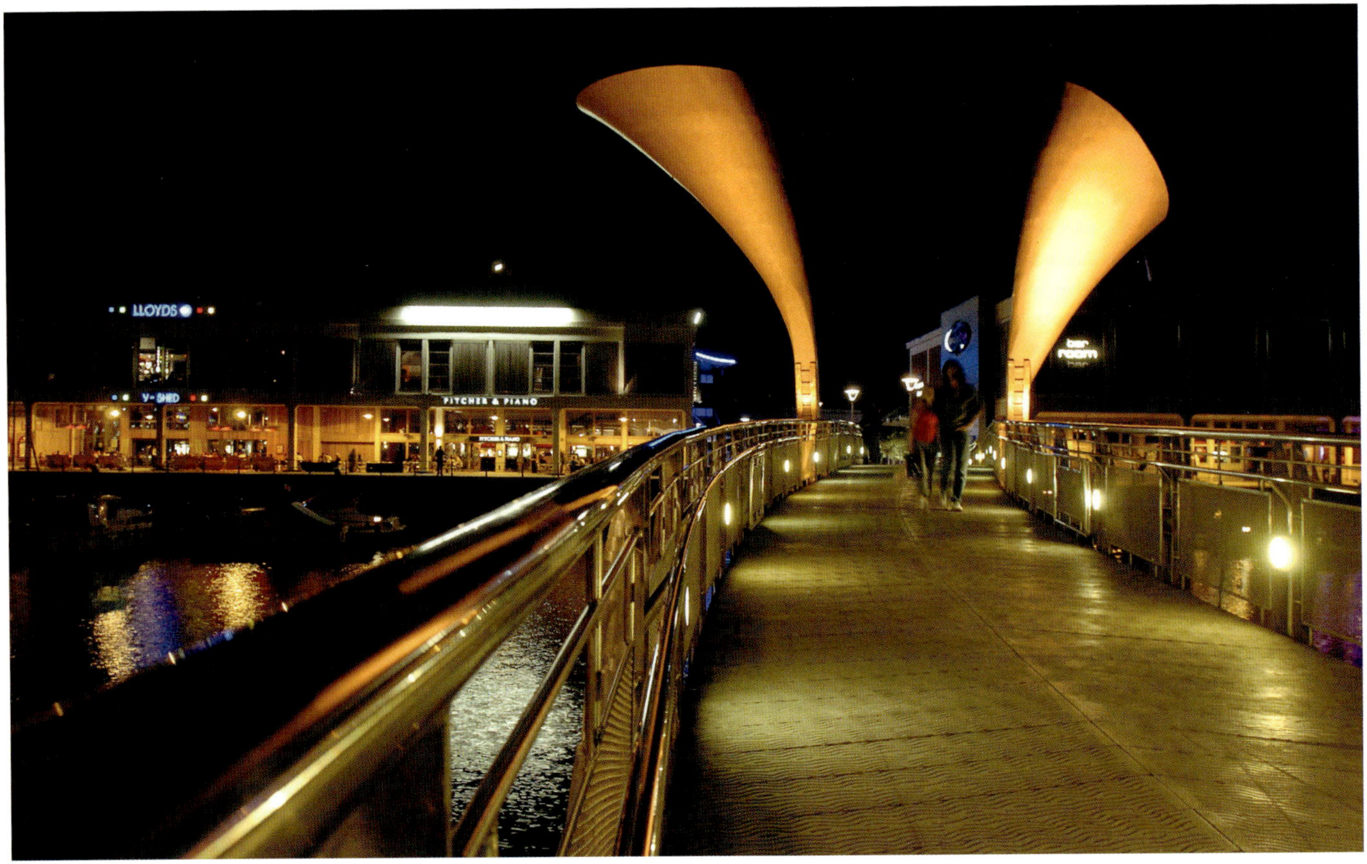

Pero's Bridge, St Augustine's Reach, is one of Bristol's newest bridges. It was named after Pero Jones, an enslaved African owned by a Bristol merchant in the 1700s. © Destination Bristol

M Shed Souvenir Guide

ISBN 9781909446175

Compiled by Gail Boyle

Based on original writing and research undertaken by staff, volunteers, academics and others engaged on the M Shed project.

First published in 2019
by Bristol Books

Bristol Books CIC, The Courtyard, Wraxall Hill, Wraxall, Bristol, BS48 1NA

Design: Joe Burt

Cover image by Jim Cossey, courtesy Destination Bristol.

Photography by David Emeney, Bristol Culture staff and volunteers (except where credited).

A CIP record for this book is available from the British Library.

M shed

BRISTOL BOOKS